super-cute
pincushions

super-cute
pincushions

35 adorable pincushions
all stitchers will love

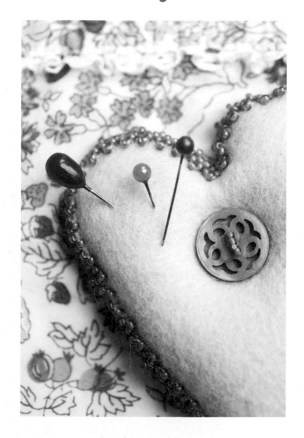

Kate Haxell

CICO BOOKS
LONDON NEW YORK

For Viv,
my sewing friend

Published in 2012 by CICO Books
An imprint of Ryland Peters & Small Ltd
20–21 Jockey's Fields, London WC1R 4BW
519 Broadway, 5th Floor, New York, NY 10012

www.cicobooks.com

10 9 8 7 6 5 4 3 2 1

Text © Kate Haxell 2012
Design and photography © CICO Books 2012

A CIP catalog record for this book is available
from the Library of Congress and the British
Library.

ISBN: 978 1 908170 30 9
Printed in China

Editor: Sarah Hoggett
Designer: Mark Latter
Photographers: Claire Richardson,
Emma Mitchell, Geoff Dann
Illustrator: Stephen Dew
Stylist: Sophie Martell

For digital editions, visit
www.cicobooks.com/apps.php

contents

introduction

I learned to sew as a small child and my first pincushion was a red fabric dome with a circle of little Chinese men dressed in rainbow colors holding hands around it. I loved it and named all the men with wobbly writing on the base. For a reason that made perfect sense then, but now entirely escapes me, all their names began with J: John, Joseph, Jim, James, Jake, Julian…

Like many stitchers, I love to have pretty tools—but it has to be practical, as well as pretty. I do various kinds of sewing and have ended up with a collection of different pincushions, each perfect for the task in hand. My two sewing machines—and my embellisher machine—all wear padded belts (see page 84) that are right there when you need to take out a pin without taking your eyes off what you are sewing. For hand-sewing I have a magnetic pincushion (see page 86), which is also brilliant for finding the needle I inevitably drop at some point: I wave the pincushion like a wand and magically my needle reappears. I go to study at the Royal School of Needlework at Hampton Court Palace once a week, and my needle-and-pin book (see page 75) goes with me. In fact, I have a pair of books (a tiny library), one for pins, one for needles. For pinning clothes for alterations I wear a wrist pincushion (see page 72), and a pea pod (see page 108) lives in the spare bedroom along with a few other sewing bits visiting friends might need. I have a cupcake jar (see page 70) for my knitting pins (I'm one of those few people who like sewing up their knitting projects almost as much as they like knitting them), and the blunt-tipped needles live in the jar itself. I have a few other pincushions besides, but I think I'm starting to sound a bit geeky…

The simple fact is that a pincushion, like any other piece of equipment, should be fit for purpose—you shouldn't have to sew with something that doesn't suit you. And the filling is important, too. A carborundum or sand-filled pincushion will keep pins sharp and bright (essential if you don't sew very often), and you'll find a note with each project recommending the best fillings for it.

Needless to say, I've loved doing this book; it's been the perfect outlet for my pincushion nerdiness. I hope that one of these 35 cute but practical projects is the perfect pincushion for you.

Kate Haxell

pincushion pets

Little ladybug ✳ My dinosaur ✳ Wide-eyed owl

Patchwork tortoise ✳ Big-eared bunnies ✳ Mrs Mouse

Home-sew hedgehog

little **ladybug**

Bright and cheerful, this is an excellent pincushion for a child to help make and then to have as their own. Start them stitching at a young age!

you will need

Ladybug templates (page 117)

Scissors, needles, and pins

Two 4 x 2-in. (10 x 5-cm) and one 3½ x 2¾-in. (9 x 7-cm) piece of red wool/acrylic mix felt

Small pieces of black felt

Fading fabric marker pen

Fabric glue

Sewing threads to match felts

Two tiny pearl buttons

Two flat black beads

3½ x 2¾-in. (9 x 7-cm) piece of cardboard

Kapok stuffing

Blunt-pointed knitting needle or thin chopstick

 1 Using the templates on page 117, cut two bodies and one base from red felt, and two heads from black felt. Cut as many spots as you want from black felt. Using small dabs of fabric glue, stick the heads in position as indicated by the dotted line on the body template; note that the top and bottom edges of the head should just stick out beyond the edge of the body, as shown far right. Use dabs of glue to stick the spots in place, remembering that ladybugs are symmetrical.

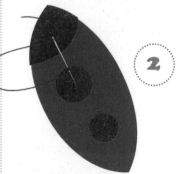

2 Using black sewing thread, blanket stitch (see page 111) around each spot and along the edge of the head that curves across the body.

 3 Using a beading needle and black sewing thread, sew a button to each head piece, then sew a bead to the middle of each button, positioning them as shown to make the eyes.

choosing colors My ladybug is the classic red model with black spots, but they can be black with red spots, orange with black spots, or orange with white spots. You can, of course, make your ladybug purple with green spots if those are your favorite colors.

 4 Put the two body pieces wrong sides together. Using black sewing thread, blanket stitch from the nose to the back of the head and fasten off. Using red sewing thread, blanket stitch along the top of the body.

stuffing the pincushion

This pincushion is stuffed with kapok, though you could use polyester fiber or wool roving if you prefer (see page 115).

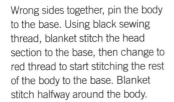

5 Wrong sides together, pin the body to the base. Using black sewing thread, blanket stitch the head section to the base, then change to red thread to start stitching the rest of the body to the base. Blanket stitch halfway around the body.

6 Cut a base from cardboard, trim it a little and slip it into the ladybug. Sew up the seam a bit more, stuff the ladybug quite firmly with kapok, then finish sewing the body to the base.

my dinosaur

I chose the bits I liked best from different dinosaurs to make my own beast—bumpy head, magnificent spikes, pointy teeth, and big claws. But he's really very amiable...

you will need

Dinosaur templates (page 117)

Scissors, needles, and pins

Two 6¼ x 4-in. (16 x 10-cm), one 3 x 2½-in. (8 x 6-cm) piece of green wool/acrylic mix felt, and two 2½ x 2½-in. (6 x 6-cm) pieces in a darker tone

Scraps of cream and blue felt

Fading fabric marker pen

Sewing thread to match darker felt and cream and blue felts

Two black delica beads

Dark brown stranded embroidery floss (thread)

Variegated green wool/acrylic machine embroidery thread

Kapok stuffing

Blunt-pointed knitting needle or thin chopstick

3 x 2½ in. (8 x 6 cm) piece of cardboard

 1 Using the templates on page 117, draw around the body onto the largest pieces of felt and cut out two shapes. Cut out the spike section from the template along the dotted line, draw around it onto the darker pieces of felt, and cut out two shapes. Cut one base from the remaining piece of felt. Cut out the eyes, teeth, and claws from cream felt and the irises from blue felt.

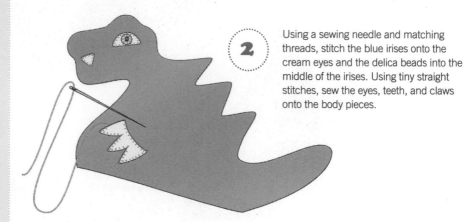

 2 Using a sewing needle and matching threads, stitch the blue irises onto the cream eyes and the delica beads into the middle of the irises. Using tiny straight stitches, sew the eyes, teeth, and claws onto the body pieces.

3 Using an embroidery needle and two strands of dark brown embroidery floss (thread), embroider the mouth with lines of chain stitch (see page 112) and the nostrils with single detached chain stitches (see page 113).

4 Using matching sewing thread, whip stitch (see page 111) the two spike pieces right sides together along the straight edge.

5 Pin one side of the spike section wrong sides together to one body piece. Thread a fine embroidery needle with a long length of variegated thread. Starting at the back of the neck, blanket stitch (see page 111) the spikes to the body. When you get to the end of the spike section, pin the other body section wrong sides together to the other side of the spike section. Make a single blanket stitch to anchor the two body pieces together, then blanket stitch the other side of the spikes.

6 When you get back to the head, continue blanket stitching to sew the two body pieces together around the head to under the chin. Do not fasten off the thread. Stuff the head and the spikes firmly with kapok, using the knitting needle or chopstick to push it right in to the corners, then continue blanket stitching down to the bottom edge of the body.

7 Go back to the far end of the spikes and blanket stitch around the tail, stuffing it as you go.

8 Fit the base into the bottom of the dinosaur body and blanket stitch halfway around it. Stuff the rest of the dinosaur with kapok. Cut a base from the cardboard and trim it down by ⅛ in. (3 mm) all around. Slide it into the dinosaur to sit on the felt base, then complete the blanket stitching.

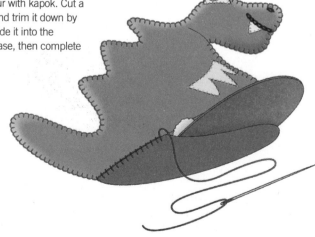

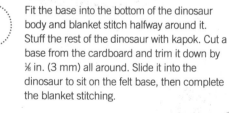

stuffing the pincushion
This pincushion is stuffed with kapok, packed in to make it firm (see page 115).

wide-eyed **owl**

This perky and practical owl will bring personality to your sewing table, and his sand-filled body will help keep your pins bright and sharp.

1 Using the templates on page 118, cut two heads and one wing piece from pale orange felt. Sandwich the remaining piece of pale orange felt in half with the fusible bonding web and cut one base from this stiffened felt. Cut two large eyes from green felt, two small eyes from blue felt, and one beak from orange felt. Cut two bodies from cotton fabric.

2 Pin the fabric body pieces right sides together. Set the sewing machine to a small straight stitch and, taking a ½-in. (1-cm) seam allowance, sew the curved side seams. Clip and press the seams (see page 116), then turn the body right side out. Turn under and fingerpress a narrow hem around the bottom edge.

3 Match the center back of the wing piece to the center back of the body, about ½ in. (1 cm) above the bottom edge. Wrap the wing piece around the body and pin it in place—you may find it easier to baste (tack) it at this stage. Thread a needle with crewel wool, and blanket stitch (see page 111) around the wing. Make the stitches irregular in length, fanning them around the curves.

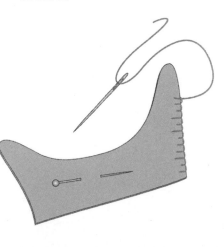

4 Pin the two felt head pieces together. Thread a needle with a long length of crewel wool and, starting at one side, blanket stitch up the side of one ear. Make the stitches quite tightly spaced but irregular in length. Toward the top of the ear, stop stitching but do not fasten off the wool.

you will need

Owl templates (page 118)

Scissors, needles, and pins

Two 3 x 2-in. (8 x 5-cm), one 4 x 1¾-in. (10 x 4.5-cm), and one 2 x 2-in. (5 x 5-cm) piece of pale orange wool/acrylic mix felt

2 x 2-in. (5 x 5-cm) piece of fusible bonding web

Small pieces of green, pale blue, and orange wool/acrylic mix felt

Two 4 x 3-in. (10 x 8-cm) pieces of printed cotton fabric

Fading fabric marker pen

Crewel wools to tone with fabric

Sewing machine

Sewing threads

Kapok stuffing

Fine sand

Blunt-pointed knitting needle or thin chopstick

Fabric glue

6 in. (15 cm) of baby rick-rack

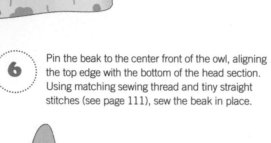

5 Matching the blanket-stitched seam of the head piece with one side seam of the body, pin then baste (tack) the front of the head to the front of the body, and the back of the head to the back of the body, with the felt overlapping the fabric by ¼ in. (5 mm). Starting at the open end of one side of the head, blanket stitch the head to the body with crewel wool, making the stitches irregular in length as before.

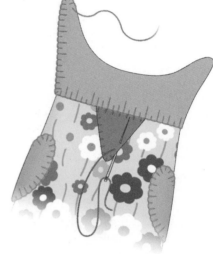

6 Pin the beak to the center front of the owl, aligning the top edge with the bottom of the head section. Using matching sewing thread and tiny straight stitches (see page 111), sew the beak in place.

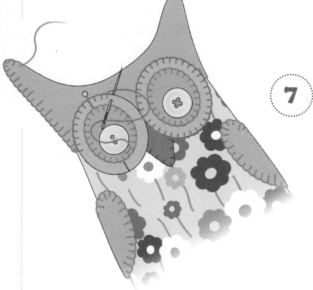

7 Stack one smaller eye on one larger one and blanket stitch them together with crewel wool, making the stitches small and regular. Sew a button to the smaller eye. Make up the other eye in the same way. Center the eyes on the beak, butt them up together, and pin in place. Using crewel wool and small, even stitches, blanket stitch the eyes in place.

8 Fit the base into the bottom of the owl and pin it, pushing the pins through the edge of the fabric into the stiffened felt. Using matching sewing thread and straight stitches, sew the base in place.

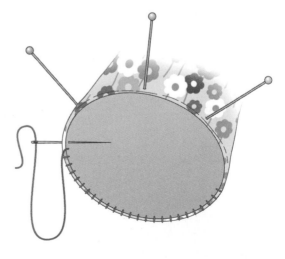

stuffing the pincushion

This pincushion is stuffed with both kapok and fine sand. The kapok fills out the shape, while the sand adds weight and keeps pins sharp (see page 115).

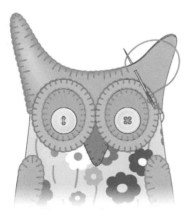

9 Put a layer of kapok into the bottom of the owl (see page 115). Fill it with fine sand to about three-quarters of the way up the body, then add more kapok. Finish blanket stitching the head, using the knitting needle or chopstick to push kapok in to fill the head and ears tightly as you sew.

10 Using small dabs of fabric glue, stick the rick-rack around the bottom edge of the owl. Match the ends at one side seam, turning them under to neaten them and securing them with a couple of tiny stitches in matching sewing thread.

patchwork **tortoise**

Classic, easy-to-sew hexagon patchwork makes the shell of this colorful tortoise. I used patches cut from different parts of the same patterned fabric so that the colors are harmonious.

you will need

Tortoise templates (page 119)

Thin paper

Scissors, needles, and pins

Two 2½ x 1½-in. (6 x 4-cm) and five 1½ x ¾-in. (4 x 2-cm) pieces of wool/acrylic mix felt

Scrap of cream felt

Fading fabric marker pen

Three colors of stranded embroidery floss (thread)

Sewing threads to match fabrics, cream felt, beads, and rick-rack

Two seed beads

Kapok stuffing

Blunt-pointed knitting needle or thin chopstick

Seven 1½ x 1½-in. (4 x 4-cm) pieces of fabric

Iron

3 x 3-in. (8 x 8-cm) piece of suedette fabric or felt

Permanent marker pen

10 in. (25 cm) of baby rick-rack

1 Using the templates on page 119, cut seven hexagons from thin paper (standard printer paper works well). Cut two heads, two front legs, two back legs, and one tail from felt. Cut two tiny circles from cream felt for eyes.

2 Using three strands of floss (thread) and a fine embroidery needle, work a small blanket stitch (see page 111) around the legs and tail, leaving the straight edges unstitched. Use one color of floss for the front legs, a second color for the back legs, and the third color for the tail. Remember to flip one of each leg piece over so that you have a left and a right leg before you embroider them.

3 Using cream sewing thread and straight stitches (see page 111), sew a cream felt circle to each head piece to make an eye—remember to flip one piece over so that you have a left and a right head before you sew on the eyes. Using matching thread, sew a bead into the center of each eye, sewing them on flat like an "O."

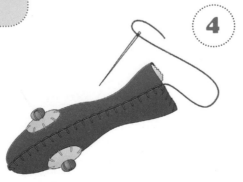

4 Pin the head pieces wrong sides together. Using three strands of the floss (thread) used for the tail and a fine embroidery needle, work a small blanket stitch all around, leaving the neck open. Stuff the head as firmly as possible with kapok, using the knitting needle or chopstick to push it right down into the nose (see page 115). Stuff the neck quite lightly, then squash the end with your fingers so that the two seams meet and whip stitch (see page 111) across the base of the neck to close it.

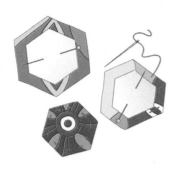

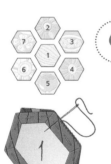

5 Pin a paper hexagon to the middle of each piece of fabric, on the wrong side. Cut out a larger hexagon, cutting about ¼ in. (5 mm) outside the paper. Thread a fine sewing needle with sewing thread. Working around each hexagon one edge at a time, fold the fabric over the paper and baste (tack) it in place.

seams You don't need to have perfectly even seam allowances all around, but don't make them much smaller or larger.

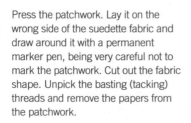

6 Arrange the hexagons with one central one and six surrounding it and number them as in the diagram (you can write the numbers on the paper on the back if you wish). Thread the needle with thread to match the fabric. Hold numbers 1 and 2 right sides together and, using tiny whip stitches, sew them along one edge.

7 Hold numbers 3 and 2 right sides together and sew along their adjoining edge, then sew 1 and 3 together along their adjoining edge. Continue in this way to add 4, 5, 6, and 7 so that the central hexagon has another hexagon sewn to each edge and the edges of adjacent hexagons are joined.

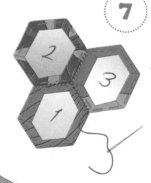

8 Press the patchwork. Lay it on the wrong side of the suedette fabric and draw around it with a permanent marker pen, being very careful not to mark the patchwork. Cut out the fabric shape. Unpick the basting (tacking) threads and remove the papers from the patchwork.

9 Wrong sides together, pin the patchwork to the suedette. Using matching sewing thread and starting at the outer edge of hexagon 2, blanket stitch the layers together along that edge. Slip a front leg into the "V" between hexagons 2 and 7 and pin it in place so that the straight edge is between the patchwork and the suedette. Blanket stitch down to the leg, then straight stitch across the leg, sewing the layers together and the leg in place at the same time. Slip a back leg into the "V" between hexagons 7 and 6, and blanket stitch down to it and straight stitch across it. Continue in this way, adding the tail, the second back leg, then the second front leg to the next three "Vs." Leaving the last "V" open, fasten off the thread.

10 Starting at the base of the open "V" and tucking the raw end under the patchwork, slip stitch (see page 111) the rick-rack to the outer edge of the patchwork shell, taking care not to stitch through the suedette. It should just overlap the edges of the patches. When you get back to the starting point, trim off any excess rick-rack leaving a ¼-in. (5-mm) tail and tuck this under the patchwork, making the join between the start and finish of the rick-rack as neat as possible.

11 Stuff the shell firmly with kapok (see page 115). Slip the flat end of the neck into the shell against the suedette base and pin it in place. Using matching thread, slip stitch the suedette to the underside of the neck. Push any more stuffing needed into the shell above the top of the neck, then slip stitch the top of the shell to the top of the neck, stitching through the edge of the patchwork under the rick-rack.

stuffing the pincushion

This pincushion is tightly stuffed with kapok to make it firm but light. You could substitute polyester fiber or wool roving if you prefer (see page 115).

big-eared bunnies

With their madly whirling eyes and oversized ears these bunnies are a bit bonkers—but their sand-filled bodies are perfect for sticking pins into.

1 Using the templates on page 119 and the fading fabric marker pen, draw a body on the ticking and on the largest piece of printed fabric, and two of each ear on the smaller pieces. Cut out the pieces. (You can draw your own ear shapes freehand to make even bigger ears.)

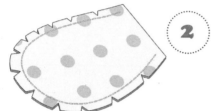

2 Pair up the ears, right sides facing. Set the sewing machine to a small straight stitch and sew from the base around the curved part of the ear, leaving the base open. Trim and notch the seam allowances (see page 116). Turn the ears right side out and press flat.

3 Embroider whipped wheel eyes (see page 114) on the ticking body. I have used stranded, pearl cotton, and wool flosses (threads) to make eyes, and they all work well. If you are using stranded floss, then three strands will probably be best. You can outline the eye with chain stitch (see page 112) if you wish, and add a tiny French knot (see page 113) nose if your bunny wants one. Cut out the body.

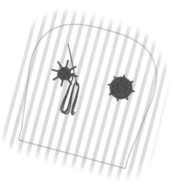

4 Right sides together, pin the ears to the body as shown, making sure that the open ends are level with the edge of the body and that none of the rest of either ear is within ⅜ in. (1 cm) of the edge of the body. Put the pins in with the tips pointing toward the base of the ears—it will be easier to take them out later.

you will need

Bunny templates (page 119)

Scissors, needles, and pins

Fading fabric marker pen

4½ x 4¼-in. (11 x 10.5-cm) piece of cotton ticking fabric

4½ x 4¼-in. (11 x 10.5-cm) piece of printed cotton fabric

Two 2½ x 3-in. (6 x 8-cm) and two 2½ x 2¾-in. (6 x 7-cm) pieces of printed cotton fabric

Sewing machine

Sewing threads to match fabric

Embroidery flosses (threads)

Two 3½ x 2-in. (9 x 5-cm) pieces of cream felt

3½ x 2-in. (9 x 5-cm) piece of fusible bonding web

Iron

Fine sand

Two buttons

Strong thread

embroidered eyes Make the eyes level or uneven, equal-sized or odd—each bunny has his own personality and most of it is expressed through his eyes. You can put the fabric into an embroidery hoop to work the eyes if you prefer; this will also help to stop the fabric from puckering.

5 Lay the printed cotton body right side down on top of the ticking body and ears, matching all edges. Taking a ⅜-in. (1-cm) seam allowance, machine-sew around the curved section of the body, leaving the straight base open. Notch the curves (see page 116) and press.

6 Turn the bunny right side out. Use the top of a knitting needle or a chopstick to carefully push out the curves and use your fingers to press the curves into the smoothest shapes possible. Turn under ⅜ in. (1 cm) around the base of the bunny and press.

7 Sandwich the two pieces of felt together with fusible bonding web to make a double-thickness piece of felt. Make sure the pieces are firmly bonded. Use the template to cut the bunny base from this felt.

8 Fit the base into the bottom of the bunny, pushing pins through the fabric into the edge of the felt to hold it in place. (Make sure the ends of the pins are pushed into the felt so that you don't catch your fingers on them while sewing.) Using small straight stitches (see page 111) and cream sewing thread, sew each base in place. Make the stitches quite deep into the felt, emerging close to the folded edge of the fabric body. Stitch around until there is just a gap large enough to spoon sand through, fill the bunny with fine sand, then complete the stitching.

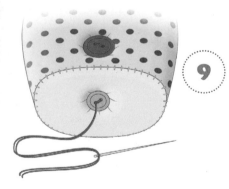

9 The bunny's tail is a button, and adding it also helps firm up the sand-filled body. Position one button on the felt base and one button on the lower back, in the right position for a tail. Using doubled strong thread, start by going through the base where the button will be and coming out through a hole in the tail button. Go down through the other hole in the tail button and come out on the base and thread on that button. Go through the buttons a few more times, pulling the thread as tight as possible while molding the sand-filled body in your hands. Fasten off the thread by knotting and looping it around the base button.

stuffing the pincushion

This pincushion is filled with fine sand to help keep your pins sharp and bright. You could use carborundum grit if you prefer (see page 115).

10 Using the same floss (thread) as for the eyes, work a line of chain stitch around the base of the bunny.

mrs mouse

Huge ears, a long nose, and an even longer tail make this mouse very cute indeed. The ears double up as needle holders; just push your needles through the felt to keep them to hand.

you will need

Mouse templates (page 119)

Scissors, needles, and pins

Two 6 x 3½-in. (15 x 9-cm) and two 2 x 2½-in. (5 x 6-cm) pieces of needlecord fabric

Scrap of cream felt

Sewing threads to match cream felt, sequins, and fabric

Two sequins

Two black delica beads

Two 2 x 2½-in. (5 x 6-cm) pieces of pink felt

Fading fabric marker pen

Stranded embroidery floss (thread) to tone with pink felt

Piece of needlecord fabric measuring 1¼ in. (3 cm) by as long as you want the tail to be, or a piece of thick cord the required length of the tail

Iron

Sewing machine

Two 2½ x 2½ -in. (6 x 6-cm) pieces of muslin (calico) fabric

Fine sand

Kapok stuffing

Blunt-pointed knitting needle or thin chopstick

Circle of pink felt with a 1⅜-in. (3-cm) radius

1 Using the templates on page 119, draw around the body and the ear onto the needlecord fabric and cut out two of each shape.

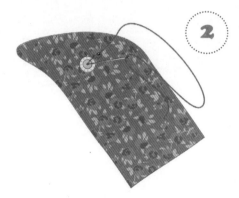

2 Cut two tiny circles from the cream felt. Using a sewing needle and matching thread and small straight stitches (see page 111), sew the circles onto the head as eyes. Bring the needle up through the center of the eye, thread on a sequin and a delica bead (change to a beading needle if need be) and, skipping the bead, take the needle back down through the sequin and the eye. Fasten off the thread on the back and repeat on the other body piece, making sure the eyes are in the same position.

3 Turn under, fingerpress, and then baste (tack) the narrowest possible hem around the edge of each fabric ear. Lay the ears on the pink felt and, using the fading fabric marker pen, draw around them. Cut out the felt ears.

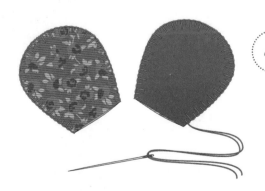

4 Right sides facing, pin a felt ear to each fabric ear. Using an embroidery needle and two strands of floss (thread), blanket stitch (see page 111) around the curved part of each ear, leaving the straight edge open. Make the stitches irregular in length, fanning them around the curves.

5 For the tail, make a rouleau tube (see page 116) from the long strip of fabric. If this sounds daunting, use a length of toning cord for the tail instead. Either turn in and stitch one end of the rouleau tube to neaten it, or tie a knot in one end of the cord.

6 Press under a ⅜-in. (1-cm) hem on the bottom edge of each body piece, then open the hems out again. Pin the body pieces right sides together.

7 From the bottom edge, slip the raw end of the tube or cord between the body pieces and out through the back seam, with the end emerging just above the pressed line. Pin or baste (tack) the end of the tail in place. Set the sewing machine to a small straight stitch and sew around the body, trapping the end of the tail in the stitching and leaving the bottom edge open. Clip notches into the seam allowances on the curves (see page 116) and trim the seam allowance around the nose.

 8 Press the stitching and turn the mouse right side out. Fold in the pressed hem around the bottom edge.

9 Pin the ears in place, using the illustration as a guide to position. Using an embroidery needle and two strands of pink floss (thread), blanket stitch across the straight edges, sewing the ears to the body.

10 Pin the pieces of muslin (calico) together and, taking a ⅜-in. (1-cm) seam allowance, sew around three sides. Turn right side out and fill the bag with sand. Oversew the top edge closed.

sewing on ears Slipping a piece of scrap paper into the mouse before you stitch on the ears will stop you from sewing through both sides of the body at the same time.

11 Stuff the mouse with kapok, packing it in tightly to make the nose and body firm—use the knitting needle or chopstick to push the stuffing right to the tip of the nose. Fill it to within 2 in. (5 cm) of the bottom edge, then push in the sandbag. Pack in more kapok around the bag to make the body smooth. Fit the base circle into the bottom of the mouse and pin it, pushing the pins through the felt. Using matching sewing thread and straight stitches, sew the base in place.

12 Using an embroidery needle and two strands of floss (thread), blanket stitch around the bottom edge of the mouse. Make the stitches quite long and irregular in length.

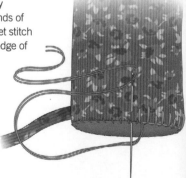

home-sew **hedgehog**

A hedgehog without spines just isn't right, so putting pins into this little pet makes him very happy!

1 Using the templates on page 120, cut two bodies, one base, and two ears from dark brown felt and two bodies and one base from black interfacing; set the interfacing pieces aside. Cut two tiny circles of cream felt for the eyes.

2 Using cream sewing thread, a fine needle, and tiny straight stitches (see page 111), sew one eye to each body piece. Remember to flip one piece over so that you have a left and a right body before you sew on the eyes. Sew a black bead onto each cream circle to complete the eyes.

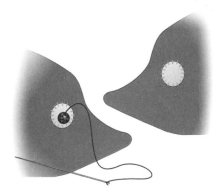

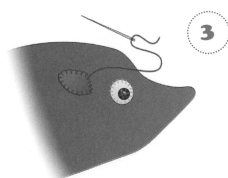

3 Using dark brown sewing thread and starting at one corner, blanket stitch (see page 111) around the curve of each ear; do not fasten off the thread. Pin an ear to each body, just behind the eye, then straight stitch the ear to the body across the straight edge.

you will need

Hedgehog templates (see page 120)

Two 4 x 2-in. (10 x 5-cm) and one 2½ x 1⅜-in. (6 x 3.5-cm) piece of dark brown wool/acrylic mix felt

Two 4 x 2-in. (10 x 5-cm) and one 2½ x 1⅜-in. (6 x 3.5-cm) piece of black iron-on lightweight interfacing

Scissors, needles, and pins

Scrap of cream felt

Fading fabric marker pen

Cream, black, and dark brown sewing threads

Two faceted black beads

Black and three shades of brown embroidery flosses (threads)

Iron

Polyester fiber stuffing

Blunt-pointed knitting needle or thin chopstick

Carborundum grit

stuffing the pincushion

This pincushion is filled with carborundum grit to keep your pins sharp (see page 115). The weight also makes the hedgehog sit solidly on your worktable, ready for when you need him. You'll also need a little polyester stuffing for the nose and head.

4 Using three strands of embroidery floss (thread) and a fine embroidery needle, work straight stitches in all three shades of brown on both body pieces. Start the stitches level with the ears and mix stitch lengths and colors as you work back across the body.

5 Iron one interfacing piece to the back of each felt body and base piece. Using dark brown sewing thread and a small blanket stitch, sew the body pieces together from the marked point under the chin on the template to the top of the forehead. Stop stitching, but do not fasten off the thread.

6 Using three strands of black embroidery floss (thread), work satin stitches (see page 114) across the tip of the snout to make the nose, fastening off the floss on the inside. Continue blanket stitching the bodies together until you get to the marked point under the bottom.

7 Pin the base piece into the opening between the chin and bottom. Blanket stitch as before from the bottom around to the chin and halfway down the other side of the base.

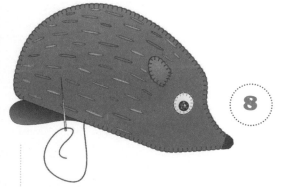

8 Stuff the nose and head with polyester stuffing, using the knitting needle or chopstick to poke it right down to the tip of the nose (see page 115). Fill the body with carborundum grit until it is as full as you can get it. Use the knitting needle or chopstick to stuff a little more polyester stuffing into the gap until the body is packed firm, then complete the blanket stitching.

quirky but cute

Spiky cactus ✳ Matryoshka dolls ✳ Bottle-cap pincushion

Chubby alien ✳ Day of the Dead ✳ Beaded pincushion pot

spiky **cactus**

Such an obvious choice for a pincushion, as it actually looks better with pins stuck into it. And it's really, really easy to make. You can make your cactus fit a larger pot simply by enlarging the template to a different size.

you will need

Cactus template (page 120)

Scissors, needles, and pins

Two 6 x 4-in. (15 x 10-cm) pieces of green wool/acrylic mix felt

Scraps of red wool/acrylic mix felt

Red sewing thread

Red seed beads

Stranded embroidery floss (thread) to match green felt

Kapok stuffing

Blunt-pointed knitting needle or thin chopstick

Mini flower pot measuring 1¾ in. (4.5 cm) across the top and 1½ in. (4 cm) high

12 x 1¼-in. (30 x 3-cm) strip of brown felt

All-purpose glue

Scrap of cardboard (optional)

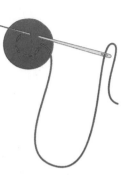

 1 Using the template on page 120, two cactus shapes from green felt. Cut as many small circles of red felt as you would like flowers; each circle should be about ¼ in. (5 mm) across. Using a fine sewing needle and red thread, work a small circle of tiny running stitches (see page 110) in the middle of a red felt circle.

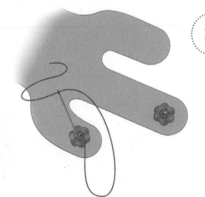

 2 Pull the stitches up tight to make a little flower. Sew the flower to one of the green cactus pieces with a couple of tiny stitches. Then bring the needle up through the middle of the flower, thread on a seed bead, and go back down through the flower. Fasten off the thread on the back. Repeat Steps 1 and 2 with the other felt circles.

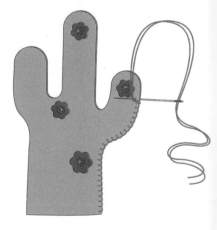

 3 Pin the cactus pieces wrong sides together. Using an embroidery needle and two strands of floss (thread) and starting at one bottom edge, blanket stitch (see page 111) up one side of the cactus.

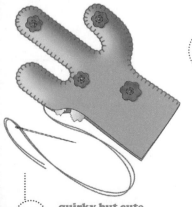

4 Continue stitching around the arms of the cactus, stuffing them firmly with kapok as you go—use the knitting needle or chopstick to push stuffing right into the tips. Stitch right down to the bottom on the other side of the trunk and fasten off the floss (thread). Stuff the trunk of the cactus.

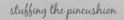
stuffing the pincushion
This pincushion is stuffed with kapok, packed in to make it firm (see page 115).

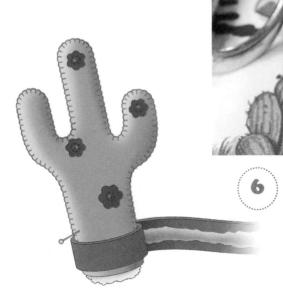

5 Stand the cactus in the flower pot and put a pin in the trunk to mark where the edge of the flower pot comes up to.

6 Spread some glue on the strip of felt and roll it around the base of the cactus, just below the pin. Leave the glue to dry completely, then remove the pin.

planting your cactus
The number of times you need to wrap the felt around the base of the cactus to make it fit in the pot will vary depending on the pot you have. Experiment by taping the wrapping in place and fitting it into the pot before you glue it on.

7 If there is a hole in the base of your flowerpot, glue a circle of cardboard over it inside the pot. Spread some glue around the inside of the pot, but not higher than ⅜ in. (1 cm) below the rim. Push the cactus into the pot so that the brown felt wrapping is just below the rim of the pot. Leave the glue to dry.

spiky cactus

matryoshka **dolls**

I chose the same fabric in three different colorways to make these little dolls, but you can make them all the same color and just vary the floss (thread) colors if you prefer.

you will need

Doll templates (page 121)

Scissors, needles, and pins

Fading fabric marker pen

Three 1¼ x 1¼-in. (3 x 3-cm) pieces of cream felt

Two 3½ x 3-in. (9 x 8-cm), two 4 x 3½-in. (10 x 9-cm), and two 4¾ x 4½-in. (12 x 11-cm) pieces of cotton fabric

Stranded embroidery flosses (threads)

Sewing machine

Sewing threads to match felt and fabrics

Iron

Blunt-pointed knitting needle or thin chopstick

Two 5½ x 1½-in. (14 x 4-cm) pieces of cream felt

5½ x 1½-in. (14 x 4-cm) piece of fusible bonding web

Kapok stuffing, fine sand, and carborundum grit

 1 Using the templates on page 121, draw around the faces on the squares of cream felt, and the bodies on the cotton fabrics. (For the front of each doll, it will be useful to draw both the outer line and the dashed stitching line of the body pieces onto the cotton fabric.) You need one face and two body pieces for each doll.

 2 Transfer the features onto the faces (see page 110). Using two strands of floss (thread), embroider the features (see box, opposite, and pages 110–114). Carefully cut out the faces, and the body pieces.

 3 Position each face on a fabric body and sew it in place with tiny straight stitches (see page 111) in cream sewing thread. Using three strands of yellow floss (thread) for the larger two dolls and two strands for the tiny doll, embroider the hair with tightly packed rows of stem stitch (see page 114).

4 Embroider a line of stem stitch in yellow around the outer edge of the hair section. Then use stem stitch and three strands of blue floss (thread) to embroider the ends of the headscarf and a line right around the face.

stitching the features

It can be tricky to embroider such tiny features, but don't obsess about making them perfect. As you sew each face, each doll will develop its own personality; my largest doll has a distinctly naughty face, while the smallest one looks rather saintly. The middle-sized one looks surprised to have such different sisters. The stitches I used are:

Eye outlines: stem stitch and blanket stitch in brown.
Irises: concentric circles of chain stitch in pale green.
Pupils and nostrils: French knots in brown.
Cheeks: straight-stitch stars in pink.
Mouths: backstitch in pink.

5 Pin the two body pieces for each size of doll right sides together. Set the sewing machine to a small straight stitch. Taking a ⅜-in. (1-cm) seam allowance, sew around the shaped sides of the body, leaving the straight base open. Clip the curves (see page 116) and press the seams, taking care not to press the embroidered section.

6 Turn the dolls right side out. Use the top of a knitting needle or a thin chopstick to carefully push out the curves, and use your fingers to press the curves into the smoothest shapes possible. Turn under ⅜ in. (1 cm) around the base of each doll and press with the iron.

stuffing the pincushions

These pincushions have different fillings to make them super-useful. The largest is filled with tightly packed kapok, the middle one with fine sand, and the smallest one with carborundum grit (see page 115).

7 Sandwich the two remaining pieces of felt together with the piece of fusible bonding web to make a double-thickness piece of felt. Make sure the pieces are firmly bonded. Use the templates to cut the doll bases from this felt.

8 Stuff each doll, filling the largest with tightly packed kapok, the middle one with fine sand, and the smallest one with carborundum grit. Push a little kapok into the base of the sand- and grit-filled dolls to prevent the filling from falling out (see page 115).

9 Fit a base into the bottom of each doll body, pushing pins through the fabric into the edge of the felt to hold it in place. (Make sure the ends of the pins are pushed into the felt so that you don't catch your fingers on them while sewing the bases in place.) Using small straight stitches and cream sewing thread, sew each base in place. Make the stitches quite deep into the felt, emerging close to the folded edge of the fabric body.

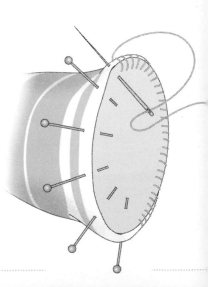

bottle-cap pincushion

Small and sweet, this mini pincushion needs only tiny bits of fabric and thread—a perfect scrap-bag project. And you're doing a bit of creative recycling at the same time!

1 Stand the bottle cap on the small piece of felt, draw around it, and cut out the circle. Set this aside.

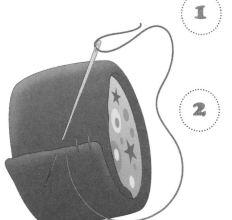

2 Wrap the strip of blanket or felt around the bottle cap, aligning one edge with the top of the cap and overlapping the ends. Using matching sewing thread and straight stitches, sew the end of the strip in place. Don't pull the strip tight; it should just fit snugly.

you will need

Soda bottle cap

Scissors, needles, and pins

Piece of felt just bigger than the top of the bottle cap

Strip of felted blanket or wool felt the circumference of the bottle cap plus ¼ in. (5 mm), by the height of the bottle cap plus ¼ in. (5 mm)

Fine woolen embroidery threads

All-purpose glue

2¾-in. (7-cm) square of felt

Sewing thread to match felt

Polyester fiber stuffing

Fading fabric marker pen (optional)

3 Fit the circle of felt cut in Step 1 onto the top of the bottle cap. Using fine woolen thread, blanket stitch (see page 111) the edge of the circle to the strip. Slip the cap out of the felt cover and finish the thread on the inside. Spread a little glue on the top of the cap, then slip the felt cover back on.

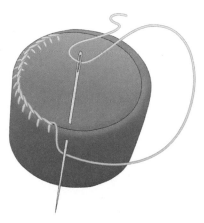

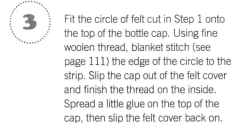

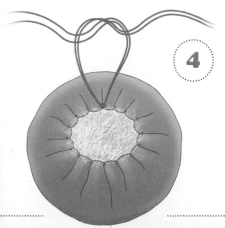

4 Cut the corners off the square of felt to make a rough circle. Using doubled sewing thread, work a small running stitch around the edges of the circle. Pull on the ends of the thread to gather the circle up a little. Stuff the circle with polyester fiber, then pull the gathers up tightly. If necessary, push in a little more stuffing to make a firm felt ball. Tie the ends of the thread in a tight knot.

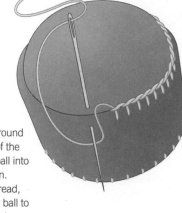

5 Spread a little glue around the inside top edge of the cap, then push the ball into it, gathered end down. Using fine woolen thread, blanket stitch the felt ball to the top edge of the strip.

starting the embroidery Knot the end of the thread, slip the needle between the felt ball and the side strip, bring it through the fabric where you want to start stitching, and pull it through so that the knot disappears. The needle will slip easily between the felt and the bottle cap, making the embroidery quick and easy to do.

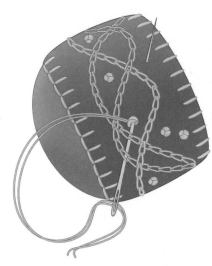

6 Using fine woolen threads, embroider a design around the side of the pincushion. You can use a fading fabric marker pen to sketch out the design if you wish. I used one strand of fine woolen thread to embroider several curving lines of chain stitch (see page 112) and two strands to work French knots (see page 113).

7 Finally, decorate the top of the felt ball with more embroidery. As before, you can use a fading fabric marker pen to sketch the design.

stuffing the pincushion
This pincushion is stuffed with polyester fiber, though you could use kapok or wool roving if you prefer (see page 115).

chubby alien

This beastie boy comes from the planet Pin, so he's quite happy to be stabbed by stitchers. He's super-simple to make; you could create a whole colony of creatures!

you will need

Alien template (page 120)

Scissors, needles, and pins

Two 5 x 5-in. (13 x 13-cm) pieces of wool/acrylic mix felt

Fading fabric marker pen

Stranded embroidery flosses (threads)

Seed beads

Three small buttons

Scrap of felted blanket or thick wool felt in contrast color

Blunt-pointed knitting needle or thin chopstick

Kapok stuffing

Beading thread to match beads

1 Using the template on page 120, draw around it on the felt and cut out two shapes.

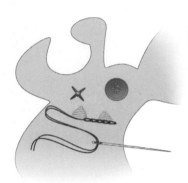

2 Embroider the face on one shape. One eye is a cross worked with three strands of floss (thread) with a seed bead sewn into the center; the other eye is a button. The mouth is worked in two strands of floss—the teeth are satin stitch (see page 114) and the mouth is a line of chain stitch (see page 114).

3 Using the template, cut a circle from the scrap of felted blanket for the tummy. Lay the circle in position on the body and, using three strands of matching floss (thread) and chain stitch, sew around the edge. Before completing the sewing, use the knitting needle or chopstick to push some stuffing under the circle, stuffing it as tight as possible. Finish the chain stitch, then work one or two more concentric circles to further define the tummy.

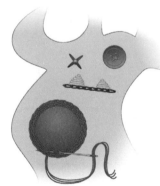

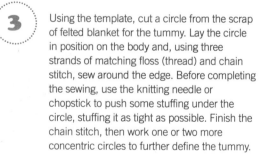

4 Pin the body pieces wrong sides together. Using two strands of floss (thread), start blanket stitching the pieces together around the head (see page 111). Stuff the horns with kapok as you sew, making them as firm as possible (see page 115).

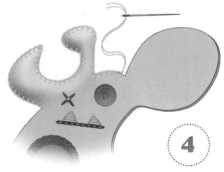

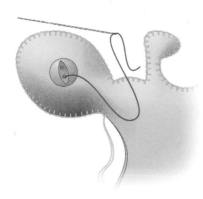

5 Sew around the third eye and stuff it, but not as firmly as the horns. Thread a beading needle with beading thread and make a stitch in the center back of the third eye. Thread on a button.

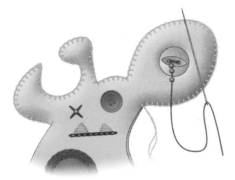

6 Take the needle through to the front of the third eye and thread on another button, then enough seed beads to span the gap between the holes in the button. Take the needle down through the other hole, through the eye, and out through the back button. Pull the thread as tight as possible. Take the needle and thread through both buttons and the beads as many times as it will fit. Finish by looping and knotting the thread firmly under the back button. Continue blanket stitching around the edge of the alien, stuffing it firmly before you complete the stitching.

stuffing the pincushion

This pincushion is stuffed with kapok, packed in to make it firm (see page 115).

day of the **dead**

This quirky pincushion is based on the decorated sugar skulls traditional to the Mexican Day of the Dead festival. Use the ribbon loop to hang the pincushion from your sewing machine, ready to hold your pins.

you will need

Iron

Four 2⅝ x 2-in. (6.5 x 5-cm) pieces of fusible interfacing

One 6 x 6-in. (15 x 15-cm) and one 2⅝ x 2-in. (6.5 x 5-cm) piece of white felt

Skull template (page 122)

Fading fabric marker pen

4-in. (10-cm) embroidery hoop

Scissors, needles, and pins

Stranded embroidery flosses (threads)

6 in. (15 cm) of ⅜-in (1-cm) double-sided satin ribbon

White sewing thread

Polyester fiber stuffing

Blunt-pointed knitting needle or thin chopstick

1 Iron one piece of fusible interfacing onto the center back of the large piece of felt. Using the template on page 122, draw the skull outline onto the area of felt backed with interfacing. Transfer the design if you wish (see page 110) and fit the felt into the embroidery hoop. Using two strands of embroidery floss (thread) unless otherwise stated, embroider the skull (see below and pages 110–114 for details of the embroidery stitches used and how to work them).

stitches used

Flamboyant color, not perfect stitching, is the key to this project. Choose your own stitches—or follow the design shown here:

Blue loops at top of forehead: individual chain stitches.
Purple curls: chain stitch.
Purple chevrons: fly stitch.
Eyes: concentric circles of orange and blue chain stitch with yellow French knots in the center, surrounded by pink individual chain stitches worked with three strands of floss (thread).
All small dots: French knots.
Nose: outlined in green chain stitch and filled in with yellow chain stitch.
Curls beside nose: blue chain stitch.
Teeth: purple blanket stitch worked with three strands of floss (thread).
Mouth: outlined in orange stem stitch.
Yellow loops on chin: individual chain stitches.
Face: outlined with orange chain stitch.

stuffing the pincushion

This pincushion is stuffed with polyester fiber packed in very tightly to make it lightweight but firm (see page 115).

2 Carefully iron a second piece of fusible interfacing to the back of the first piece, sealing in all the back of the stitching. Cut out the skull.

3 Iron two layers of interfacing to the back of the remaining piece of felt and cut out a second skull. Fold the ribbon in half to make a loop and sew the ends to the back of the plain skull—stitching through both layers of interfacing, but not the felt—with white sewing thread.

4 Pin the skulls wrong sides together. Using three strands of pink floss (thread), blanket stitch (see page 111) the skulls together, working straight stitches over the ribbon where it emerges. Before completing the stitching, stuff the skull very firmly with polyester fiber, then finish blanket stitching.

beaded pincushion pot

A glass saltcellar is turned into a little jewel of a pincushion with some beads and a charm. As these colorful gems are so small, they are surprisingly quick to make.

you will need

Glass saltcellar with screw-on lid

Paper for template

Tape measure

Ruler

Pencil

Scissors, needles, and pins

Two pieces of wool felt to fit template

Beading thread to match felt

Seed beads

Charm or large bead

Kapok stuffing

Blunt-pointed knitting needle or thin chopstick

All-purpose glue

Mini clothespins or small bulldog clips

Ribbon, yarn, or other decorative trim of your choice

 1 Measure the circumference of the lid of the saltcellar, close to the rim. Divide this measurement by two, then add ¼ in. (5 mm). Measure the depth of the lid. On paper, draw a rectangle to these measurements. On top of this, draw the shape you'd like for the top of your pincushion. Cut out two of these shapes in felt.

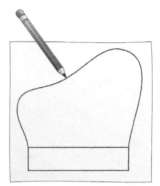

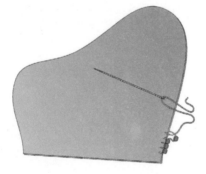

2 Place the pieces together. Using a beading needle and thread, work beaded blanket stitch (see page 112) up one side of the shape.

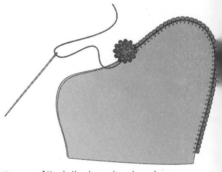

3 Attach the large bead or charm. The precise shape of your pincushion top will vary from the one shown, but the principle will be the same. How you attach the bead or charm will depend on its nature, but try to make any stitching as invisible as possible.

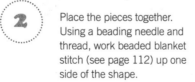

 4 Sew up the other side of the pincushion with more beaded blanket stitch. Then stuff the pincushion firmly with kapok (see page 115), leaving enough unstuffed for you to be able to slide the base of the pincushion over the saltcellar lid. Stuff it well, using the knitting needle or chopstick to push it right in. Try fitting the pincushion over the lid of the saltcellar to ensure that it will be firm enough.

stuffing the pincushion

This pincushion is stuffed with kapok, though you could use polyester fiber or wool roving if you prefer (see page 115)

variation

The blue pincushion has a more pointed shape and the rim is trimmed with chenille yarn. Spread the glue on the felt over the area to be covered, then wind the yarn on firmly over the glue.

5 Spread a thin layer of glue around the edge of the lid of the salt cellar. Slide the stuffed felt pincushion over the lid and hold it in place with mini clothespins or small bulldog clips while the glue dries.

6 Finally, glue ribbon or a decorative trim around the base of the stuffed section to cover the join between the felt and the metal lid. Neaten the ends by turning them under and gluing them down before gluing the ribbon in place.

retro style

 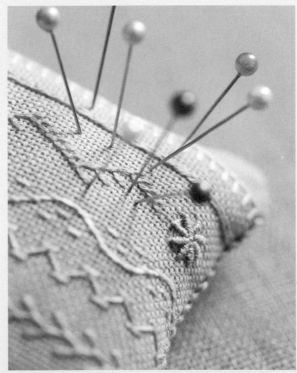

I love sewing ✳ Pretty teacup ✳ Crazy patchwork

Christmas tree ✳ Pincushion stack ✳ Bargello butterfly

Yo-yo cushion ✳ Stitch sampler

I love sewing

These delicately pretty hearts have a beaded edge that looks intricate, but is actually very easy to work.

you will need

Heart template (page 122)

Fading fabric marker pen

Scissors, needles, and pins

Two 4 x 3-in. (10 x 8-cm) pieces of wool/acrylic mix felt

Beading thread to match fabric

Seed beads

Carborundum grit

Two small buttons

1 Using the template on page 122, cut two heart shapes from the felt and pin them together. Using a beading needle and thread and starting at the base of the dip in the top of the heart, work double beaded blanket stitch (see page 112) around the shape. When you have almost reached the beginning of the beading again, fill the heart with carborundum grit. Fill it as much as possible, then complete the stitching.

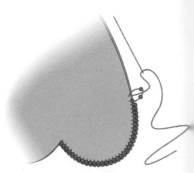

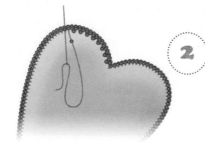

2 Thread the beading needle with a long length of thread and secure it to the beading already worked. Take the needle out through one of the inner row of beads, thread on another bead, then take the needle through the next bead along on the inner row. Bring it out through the next bead on the same row and repeat the process right around the heart.

3 To finish the beaded edge, take the needle through two beads in the outer row of beading, thread on another bead, then take the needle through the next two beads along. Repeat this right around the heart.

4 Thread the beading needle with beading thread, double it, and knot the ends. From the back, thread the needle though one hole of the button that is going to be on the back of the heart, then back down through the other hole. Take the needle between the strands of thread and pull the loop tight around the middle of the button. Push the needle right through the heart where you want the buttons to be.

variation

You can make these hearts different sizes by the simple expedient of enlarging the template to different percentages. This one is made from teal felt and is trimmed with the same beads and buttons as the main project.

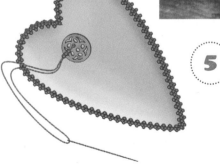

5 Thread on the other button. Thread on enough seed beads to span the gap between the holes in the button, then take the needle down through the other hole, through the heart, and out through the back button. Pull the thread as tight as possible. Mold and squash the felt with your fingers, pulling the thread tighter all the time, until the heart is firm and compact.

stuffing the pincushion
This pincushion is filled with carborundum grit, though you could use fine sand if you prefer (see page 115).

6 Take the needle and thread through both buttons and the beads as many times as it will fit. Finish by looping and knotting the thread firmly under the back button.

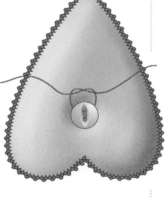

pretty **teacup**

This is absolutely the simplest pincushion to make, and is a perfect way of recycling lovely cups whose saucers have been broken. If you do have the saucer, glue it to the bottom of the cup and stash your spools of thread on it while you sew a project.

you will need

Scissors, needles, and pins

Strong sewing thread

Circle of fabric twice the diameter of the top of the teacup

Polyester fiber stuffing

Teacup

All-purpose glue

Marabou trim the circumference of the rim of the teacup

Knitting needle or lollipop stick

1 Using a sewing needle and doubled thread, work a line of running stitches (see page 110) around the circle of fabric, ¼ in. (5 mm) in from the edge. Pulling on both ends of the threads, pull the stitches up to make a pouch. Fill the pouch with as much polyester stuffing as you can push in, then pull the stitches up tight to make a fabric ball. Knot the ends of the threads, then make several stitches across the gathers to completely close the ball.

variation

This cup has a pom-pom trim around the edge instead of feathers. The trim is glued on in a similar way, with the flat part of the trim being pushed into the gap between the ball and the cup.

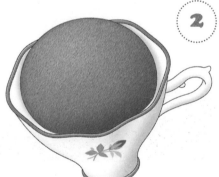

2 Push the ball into the cup, gathered side down, to check that it fits. There is no rule as to how much of the ball should stick out of the top of the cup; whatever looks best with your cup. Remove the ball and spread plenty of glue around the inside of the cup, keeping it at least ⅜ in. (1 cm) below where the top edge of the fabric ball will be. Press the ball back into the cup and leave the glue to dry.

3 Working on a short section at a time, pull the ball away from the side of the cup and squeeze some glue into the gap. Push the feather trim down into the gap, pushing it in with a knitting needle or lollipop stick. Glue the trim in all around the edge of the ball, then leave the glue to dry.

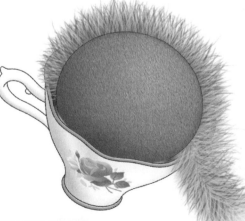

stuffing the pincushion

This pincushion is stuffed with polyester fiber, though you could use kapok or wool roving if you prefer (see page 115).

crazy patchwork

Made using an easy-to-work version of a very traditional technique, this lusciously embroidered and embellished pincushion is packed with vintage charm.

you will need

Ruler

Permanent marker pen

Piece of muslin (calico) fabric measuring at least 6 x 4½ in. (15 x 11 cm)

Scissors, needles, and pins

Scraps of fabrics, ribbons, and trims in chosen colors

Sewing threads to match fabrics

Iron

Coton à broder or stranded embroidery flosses (threads) in chosen colors

Selection of beads, buttons, sequins, and charms in chosen colors

Piece of thick fabric measuring 6 x 4½ in. (15 x 11 cm)

Sewing machine

Kapok stuffing

Blunt-pointed knitting needle or thin chopstick

 1 Using the ruler and permanent marker, draw a 6 x 4½-in. (15 x 11-cm) rectangle on the calico. Inside this, mark ⅝-in. (1.5-cm) seam allowances. Starting at one corner, pin the patches of fabric to the muslin (calico). Turn under narrow hems on fraying patches that overlap, but leave underlaps and non-fraying edges raw to reduce bulk.

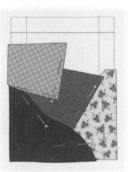

2 Using a sewing needle and matching thread, slip stitch (see page 111) along all the seams, stitching through all layers of fabric. Take out the pins as you go. Work a line of basting (tacking) stitches around the outer edges of the patchwork to hold the fabrics in place. Press the patchwork.

 3 Pin ribbons and trims to the patchwork. They can cover some seam lines or run across larger patches—whatever looks good. Using coton à broder or three strands of stranded floss (thread) and a fine embroidery needle, embroider over the visible seams with a variety of stitches and shades—this pincushion uses chain stitch, blanket stitch, feather stitch, straight stitch, and whipped running stitch (see pages 110–113).

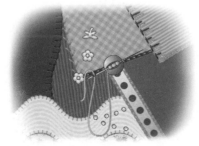

 4 Sew on the ribbons and trims, using embroidery floss (thread) or sewing thread (depending on what looks best) and decorative embroidery stitches. Sew on a selection of buttons, beads, sequins, and charms. Make sure you stitch through all the layers of fabric and keep all the embellishments at least ⅝ in. (1.5 cm) in from the edges of the patchwork.

embroidering the pincushion

If you prefer, work on a larger piece of muslin (calico) and fit it into an embroidery hoop to work the decorative stitching. This will help to stop the patchwork from puckering.

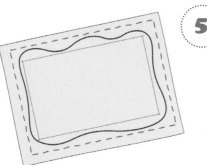

5 Cut out the muslin (calico) along the outer edges drawn in Step 1. Lay the patchwork face down, so that you can see the stitching and the marked inner seam lines on the back of the muslin (calico). Using the permanent marker pen, draw a wavy shape that lies between the outer edge and inner seam lines and doesn't cut through any of the hard embellishments. Don't make the curves too tight or they will be difficult to sew and to turn out neatly.

6 Right sides together, pin the patchwork to the piece of thick fabric. Baste (tack) around, just outside the drawn wavy line. Set the sewing machine to a medium straight stitch and machine around the wavy line, leaving a 2-in. (5-cm) gap in one edge. Turn the pincushion right side out through the gap and carefully press the seam, avoiding the hard embellishments. Press under the edges of the gap. Stuff the pincushion firmly. Sew up the gap with ladder stitch (see page 111). Thread a charm onto a short piece of ribbon, slip the ends of the ribbon into the gap, and stitch them in place as you sew the gap closed.

christmas tree

Perfect as a holiday gift for a stitcher, this Scandinavian-style Christmas tree pincushion will be beautifully useful all year round. You can trim your tree with beads, charms, or lengths of sparkly trim if you prefer.

you will need

Pencil, ruler, and paper for template

Scissors, needles, and pins

Fading fabric marker pen

Two 6¼ x 3½-in. (16 x 9-cm) pieces of leaf-green wool/acrylic mix felt

Heart template (page 123)

Two 2 x 2-in. (5 x 5-cm) pieces of pale lime-green wool/acrylic mix felt

Teal rayon thread

Selection of tiny mother-of-pearl buttons and sequins

Teal seed beads

Leaf-green stranded embroidery floss (thread)

Metal washer 1¼ in. (3 cm) in diameter

Two 2-in. (5-cm) circles of leaf-green wool/acrylic mix felt

Fabric glue

Kapok stuffing

Blunt-pointed knitting needle or thin chopstick

 On paper, draw a triangle measuring 3 in. (8 cm) across the base and 6 in. (15 cm) from base to tip. Cut this out and use it as a template to cut two triangles from leaf-green felt. Using the heart template on page 123, cut two hearts from pale lime-green felt. Pin a heart to each triangle, following the photograph for position. Using teal rayon thread and a fine sewing needle, blanket stitch (see page 111) the hearts to the triangles.

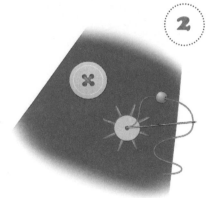

 Decorate each triangle with buttons and sequins. Sew on buttons with teal rayon thread, working the stitches in a cross if the button has four holes. Using simple straight stitches and teal thread, embroider a star where you want a sequin to be. Using a beading needle if necessary, bring the needle up in the center of the star and thread on a sequin followed by a teal seed bead. Skipping the bead, take the needle back down through the sequin to attach it.

 Pin the triangles wrong sides together. Using three strands of embroidery floss (thread) and a sewing needle, blanket stitch the triangles together along the long edges.

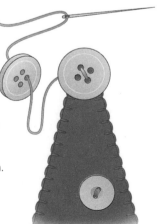

4 At the top of the tree, sew on a four-hole button on either side. Secure the teal thread in the felt, then thread on one button and stitch right through the top of the tree before threading on the other button. Work the stitches in a cross.

stuffing the pincushion

This pincushion is tightly stuffed with kapok to make it firm but light (see page 115). The metal washer in the base weights it, but you could substitute a cotton bag filled with sand or carborundum grit if you prefer.

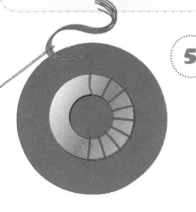

5 Using six strands of embroidery floss (thread), sew the washer to the center of one of the felt circles. Work straight stitches over the washer and right around it to hold it firmly in place. Glue the other circle to the back to cover the stitching. Leave the glue to dry.

6 Stuff the tree with kapok, using a blunt-pointed knitting needle or a chopstick to push it right into the top of the tree (see page 115).

7 Using three strands of embroidery floss (thread), blanket stitch the circle to the bottom of the tree, with the washer facing upward. Push in more stuffing as you stitch so that the tree is very firmly stuffed.

christmas tree

pincushion *stack*

This pretty vintage-style pincushion is also perfectly practical. The three pillows are filled with different materials, so you can take the best possible care of your needles and pins.

 1 Using compasses, draw on paper three circles with 1¾-in. (4.5-cm), 2¼-in. (5.5-cm), and 2⅝-in. (6.5-cm) radii. Using these as templates, cut two circles of each size from fabric. Set one circle of each size aside.

2 Using the fading fabric marker pen, draw an inner circle ⅜ in. (1 cm) smaller on the right side of one fabric circle of each size. Pin and then baste (tack) a length of rick-rack to each of these circles (shortest piece to smallest circle, etc), with the middle of the rick-rack running along the marked inner line. Position the rick-rack accurately or the final effect will be spoiled. Leave a short tail of rick-rack at the start; when you reach it again, adjust the rick-rack to make the join as neat as possible. Fold the ends away toward the edge of the circle and baste them in place.

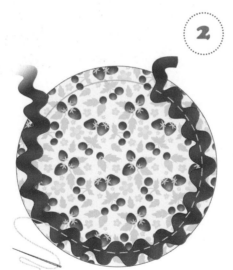

3 Right side down, lay the remaining three circles on top of the trimmed ones, matching the edges. Pin them together. Set the sewing machine to a small straight stitch. Taking a ⅜-in. (1-cm) seam allowance, carefully sew around each circle, leaving a gap for turning through. It's important that the gap does not straddle the joined ends of the rick-rack.

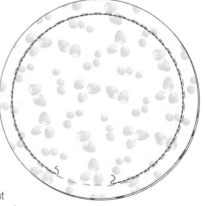

4 Turn the pillows right side out. Slip the top of a knitting needle or a chopstick inside each one and run it around the inside of the seam to press it out as smoothly as possible. Press each pillow with the iron. Stuff each pillow (see box, below, and page 115), then ladder stitch (see page 111) the gaps closed, sewing the rick-rack in place as you go.

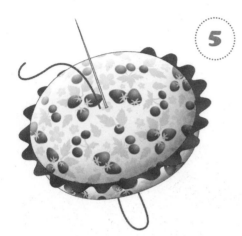

5 Thread a long, sharp needle (a doll needle is ideal) with stranded or pearl cotton floss (thread). Make a stitch through the center of the first pillow, pulling the floss through but leaving a short tail. Pull on both ends to indent the middle of the pillow as much as possible, then tie the ends in a very firm double knot. Repeat for the remaining pillows.

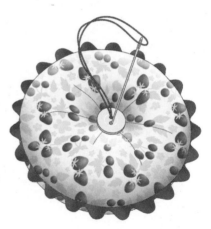

6 Thread the same needle with a long length of floss (thread), double it, and knot the ends. Take the needle through the center of the largest pillow (from top to bottom if your pillows have a defined top and bottom), then thread on a button. Take the needle through the other hole in the button and back through the center of the pillow.

7 Take the needle through the center of the middle-sized pillow, and finally the smallest pillow. Thread on the second button, then take the needle back through all three pillows and through the button on the bottom. Pull the floss (thread) as tight as you can—the tighter the better. Go back and forth through the buttons and pillows several times, finishing at the bottom button. Slip the needle through to one side of the button and secure the floss by looping and knotting it firmly under the bottom button.

> ### stuffing the pincushion
> This pincushion has three different fillings. The largest pillow is filled with tightly packed kapok, the middle one with fine sand, and the smallest one with polyester fiber (see page 115).

bargello butterfly

There is something marvelously retro about classic bargello embroidery, so in that spirit I have chosen some wonderful 1970s colors to work this pincushion in. You can, of course, choose a completely different palette if you prefer.

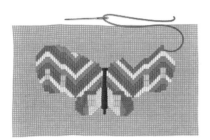

1 Following the chart on page 122, embroider the butterfly onto the canvas. Start with the body in the middle, then work the wings out to the sides. You can work the background in whatever stitch you want—I used Parisian stitch (see page 114) in colors 352 and 353. I embroidered the background to six strands of canvas larger than the butterfly all around, but you can increase this to make a larger pincushion if you prefer; remember that you may need larger pieces of canvas and needlecord fabric.

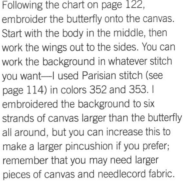

you will need

Butterfly chart (page 122)

4¾ x 7-in. (12 x 18-cm) piece of 18-count canvas

One skein each of Appleton's Crewel Wool in shades 155, 241, 352, 353, 723, 841, 932, and 934

Scissors, needles, and pins

Sewing thread to match fabric

5¾ x 3¾-in. (14.5 x 9.5-cm) piece of needlecord fabric

Polyester fiber stuffing

Tape measure

2 When the embroidery is complete, trim the canvas down to five strands larger than the embroidery all around. Fold the corners over at the edge of the embroidery, then fold the sides in to miter the corners. Catch each miter in place with a few stitches across the folded edges.

working the embroidery As this is such a small piece of canvas embroidery, you don't have to put it in a frame to work it, because it won't distort while you are stitching.

3 In the same way, fold in ⅜-in. (1-cm) seam allowances and miter the corners of the piece of needlecord fabric. (If you have made a bigger pincushion, you'll need a bigger piece of fabric. Once the edges are turned in, the fabric must be the same size as the embroidery.)

4 Using a sewing needle and matching sewing thread, whip stitch (see page 111) the needlecord fabric to the embroidery all around, leaving a small gap for stuffing. Make a small stitch through the edge of the fabric, then take the needle under the first bare strand of canvas outside the embroidery. Stuff the pincushion firmly with polyester fiber, then whip stitch the gap closed.

5 Measure around the seam line of the pincushion and add 30 percent to this measurement. Cut six strands of crewel wool to this length, two strands of each of three colors. Knot the ends and make a three-strand braid (plait), knotting the other end when the braid (plait) is finished. Using a sewing needle and thread to match the fabric, starting at the lower right-hand corner and leaving a 2-in. (5-cm) tail, sew the braid to the seam line all around the pincushion. Make a stitch through the very edge of the fabric and under the bare strand of canvas, then take the needle through the back of the braid. Pull the thread tight and repeat to sew the braid firmly in place.

6 When you get back to the starting point, join the ends of the braid with a few stitches and fasten off the yarn. Using another length of crewel wool, bind the ends of the braid together firmly. Secure the end of the yarn by stitching up and down through the binding a couple of times. Cut the ends of the braid about 1 in. (2.5 cm) from the binding and fluff them out to make a tassel.

> *stuffing the pincushion*
>
> This pincushion is stuffed with polyester fiber (see page 115), the fibers of which are least likely to work their way out through the canvas.

yo-yo cushion

This is a traditional pincushion shape made in country-style fabrics and topped with a yo-yo to complete the folksy look. You need strong floss or thread to create the segments, so choose pearl cotton or waxed linen.

you will need

Compasses

Paper for template

Scissors, needles, and pins

Fading fabric marker pen

One 4¾ x 4¾ -in. (12 x 12-cm) and one 4 x 4-in. (10 x 10-cm) piece of needlecord fabric

4¾ x 4¾-in. (12 x 12-cm) piece of blanket fabric or thick wool felt

Iron

Sewing machine

Sewing thread to match fabric

Polyester fiber stuffing

Blunt-pointed knitting needle or thin chopstick

Pearl cotton embroidery floss (thread)

Two ⅝-in. (1.5-cm) buttons and one tiny button

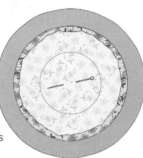

1 Using compasses, draw on paper one circle with a 2½-in. (6-cm) radius and one with a 2-in. (5-cm) radius. Using these as templates, cut one large circle and one small circle from needlecord and one large circle from blanket fabric. Draw a circle with a 1-in. (2.5-cm) radius in the center of the small needlecord circle, on the wrong side. Press under a narrow hem around the edge of the small needlecord circle. Right sides together, pin the small needlecord circle to the center of the blanket circle.

2 Set the sewing machine to a small straight stitch. Machine around the drawn line in the middle of the small circle, sewing it to the blanket circle. Pin the two larger circles right sides together. Taking a ⅜-in. (1-cm) seam allowance, sew around the outer edges, leaving a 2-in. (5-cm) gap.

3 Turn the pincushion right side out. Do not press the seam, but do press under the edges of the gap. Stuff the pincushion with polyester fiber, making it well filled but not firm. Ladder stitch the gap closed (see page 111).

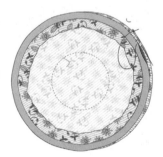

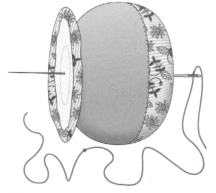

4 Cut a length (about four times the circumference of the fabric ball) of pearl cotton floss (thread) and thread a long needle; a doll needle is ideal, though a long darner will work, too. Tie a big knot in the floss 4 in. (10 cm) from the end. Push the needle right through the center of the pincushion from the needlecord side, so that it emerges in the middle of the small needlecord circle on the top. Pull the floss through to the knot.

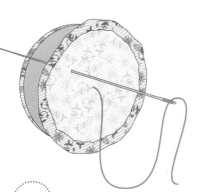

5 Take the needle through the small circle of
needlecord just beyond the line of stitching.

6 Pass the needle
around the outside
and then bring it
back up through the
center of the
pincushion in the
same place as before.
Pull the floss (thread)
as tight as possible.

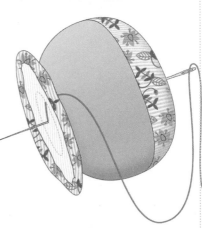

yo-yo cushion

7 Repeat the process on the opposite side of the pincushion and then at the two remaining compass points to divide the pincushion into four segments, each defined by a line of floss (thread). Pull the floss tight each time to make the segments as even as possible.

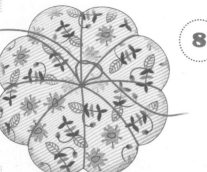

8 Repeat the process again to divide each segment in half to create a total of eight segments. Take a stitch back down through the pincushion and tie the end of the floss (thread) to the starting tail with a very firm knot.

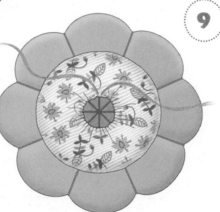

9 Thread a sewing needle with sewing thread, double it, and tie a knot 4 in. (10 cm) from the end. Starting on the right side, work running stitch (see page 110) around the turned-under hem of the small circle. Pull both ends of the threads to gather the yo-yo as tightly as possible and tie the threads in a firm knot. Thread both tails of thread into a needle, take them through to the inside of the yo-yo, and trim them short.

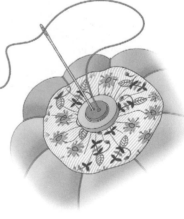

10 Thread the long needle with another length of pearl cotton floss (thread) and knot the end. From the bottom, take the needle through the center of the pincushion and up through the center of the yo-yo. Thread on a large button, then the tiny one, and then take the needle back down through the pincushion.

11 On the bottom of the pincushion, thread on the remaining button and take the needle through back up to the top. Pull the floss (thread) tight. Stitch through all the buttons a couple of times, then secure the floss by looping and knotting it under the bottom button.

stuffing the pincushion

This pincushion is stuffed with polyester fiber (see page 115), as it needs to be very spongy so that it can be pulled in by the pearl cotton floss (thread).

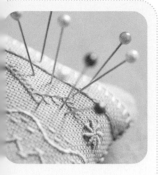

stitch sampler

Here's a version of a stitch sampler that's useful as well as pretty. You can work the stitches shown here or choose your own favorites to personalize your pincushion.

you will need

Ruler

Fading fabric marker pen

7 x 7-in. (18 x 18-cm) piece of evenweave fabric

Scissors, needles, and pins

5-in. (13-cm) embroidery hoop

Stranded embroidery flosses (threads)

Coin

4 x 4-in. (10 x 10-cm) piece of cotton fabric, cut with pinking shears

Basting (tacking) thread

Sewing machine

Sewing thread to match fabric

Cord (optional)

Polyester fiber stuffing

Blunt-pointed knitting needle or thin chopstick

 1 Using the ruler and fabric marker pen, draw a 4-in. (10-cm) square in the middle of the evenweave fabric. Fit the fabric into the hoop. Using two strands of floss (thread), embroider bands of stitches, starting ⅜ in. (1 cm) down from the top of the square and the same distance in from each edge. Start each row with a knot in the unstitched area inside the square and finish it with a few backstitches in the same area on the other side. See box, below, and pages 110–114 for embroidery stitch details.

 2 Take the fabric out of the hoop and cut out the square. On the back of the fabric, draw a 3-in. (8-cm) square centered on the stitching. Use a coin as a template to round off each of the corners.

stitches used

❖ **Blanket stitch** in yellow
❖ **Chain stitch** in lilac
❖ A **whipped wheel** in green
❖ Branching **feather stitch** in pink
❖ Three staggered rows of **running stitch** in orange, laced with yellow
❖ **Chevron stitch** in green
❖ **Feather stitch** in lilac
❖ **Open Cretan stitch** in pink

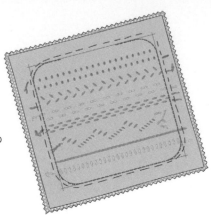

3 Pin the evenweave and cotton fabrics right sides together. Baste (tack) them just outside the marked line. Set the sewing machine to a small straight stitch and sew around the marked line, leaving a gap in one edge for turning through. Take out the basting stitches and turn the pincushion right side out. Press the corners out with your fingers, making them as smooth as possible.

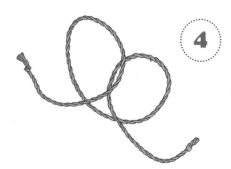

4 Either use 14 in. (35 cm) of purchased cord or make a cord from stranded floss (thread) to perfectly complement your stitching. To do this, cut two 18-in. (45-cm) lengths of each of two colors of floss. Knot all four lengths together at one end. Ask a friend to hold the knot. Divide the threads into two groups—one group of each color. Start to twist the ends of the threads, twisting each group in the same direction. When the threads are so twisted that they are beginning to kink, hold the ends together, ask your friend to let go of the knot. Let the cord coil up, then gently pull it out straight. Knot the other end.

5 Tuck one knot of the cord into the gap in the pincushion then, using sewing thread to match the fabric, sew the cord to the seam. Make a tiny stitch through the edge of the fabric, right on the seam, then make a tiny stitch through the underside of the cord, and pull the stitches tight. Continue in this way right around the pincushion. Stop when you reach the gap, but do not fasten off the thread.

stuffing the pincushion

This pincushion is stuffed with polyester fiber, as the looser fibers of kapok or roving might creep out through the evenweave fabric (see page 115).

6 Stuff the pincushion with polyester fiber, using the knitting needle or chopstick to push it right into the corners, but do not pack it in too firmly. Sew up the gap, sewing on the cord at the same time—simply make each stitch through both pieces of fabric, then through the cord. Just before you reach the end of the gap, tuck the other knot into it, then finish closing the gap, stitching under the cord. (This can be a bit tricky, but you'll get there in the end.)

perfectly **practical**

Cupcake jar pincushion ✳ Dressmaker's watch

Needle-and-pin book ✳ Fabulous finger ring

Pincushion with pockets ✳ For your sewing machine

A great gift

cupcake jar **pincushion**

These sweet and versatile pincushions look delicious and are quick, easy, and inexpensive to make. Store threads or notions in the jar and push pins into the "frosting" on top.

you will need

Compasses

Paper for template

Tape measure

Jar with a screw-top lid

Ruler

Scissors, needles, and pins

Small piece of medium-weight fabric

Fading fabric marker pen

Sewing machine

Sewing thread to match fabric

Iron

Strong glue

Polyester fiber stuffing

Blunt-pointed knitting needle or thin chopstick

Scraps of ribbon and/or trim the circumference of the jar lid

Button, charm, or beads

Fluffy yarn

Pom-pom maker

Embroidery floss (thread)

 1 Using compasses, draw on paper a circle with a radius that is the desired height of the pincushion, plus ⅜ in. (1 cm), plus the depth of the lid. Measure the circumference of the lid. Mark out this measurement plus ¾ in. (2 cm) on the edge of the circle. Draw a straight line from each end of the marked section to the center point. Cut out the shape, which will be a section of a circle.

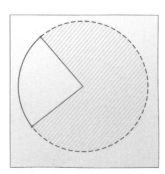

 2 Pin the template to the back of the fabric and draw around it with the fabric marker pen. Cut out the fabric shape.

 3 Right side together, fold the piece in half, matching the straight edges. Taking a ⅜-in. (1-cm) seam allowance, machine-sew up the straight sides, stopping ⅜ in. (1 cm) from the point and reversing to secure the stitching—you have made a fabric cone. Cut off the point of the cone where the seam stops. Press the seam open and turn the cone right side out.

4 Spread a layer of glue around the edge of the jar lid. Right side out, slip the lower edge of the fabric cone over the lid, easing it down over the glue and pressing it in place. Leave to dry completely.

 5 Fill the cone with polyester stuffing, (see page 115), pushing it in through the hole in the top of the cone (you'll find a blunt-pointed knitting needle or chopstick an ideal tool) and making sure it fills the cone evenly. Run a line of running stitches (see page 110) around the edge of the hole and pull it up tight. Secure the thread with some stitches across the top of the gathers.

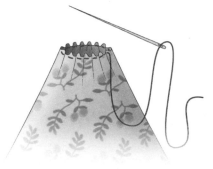

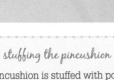

stuffing the pincushion
This pincushion is stuffed with polyester fiber to make it spongy and lightweight. You could use either kapok or wool roving if you prefer (see page 115).

6 Glue the trim around the edge of the jar lid, aligning the join in the trim with the seam in the fabric pincushion. When the glue is dry, you can glue a narrower piece of trim or ribbon over the lower edge of the first piece if you want. Using a sewing needle and thread, sew a button, beads, or a charm to the ribbon or braid to further decorate the jar.

7 Using a pom-pom maker and following the manufacturer's instructions, make a small pom-pom from fluffy yarn and tie the center of it with embroidery floss (thread), leaving long tails. Using an embroidery needle and the tails of floss, sew the pom-pom firmly to the top of the pincushion, covering the gathered top. Tie the ends of the floss in a knot under the back of the pom-pom and trim them short.

cupcake jar pincushion

dressmaker's **watch**

A wristband pincushion is perfect when pinning for alterations, and styling this one as a watch adds a cute touch. A disc of plastic in the base stops you from stabbing yourself when you push in pins.

you will need

Watch template (page 123)

Scissors, needles, and pins

2 x 2-in. (5 x 5-cm) piece of pale teal wool/acrylic mix felt

Paper for template

Compasses

Two 2½ x 2½-in. (6 x 6-cm) and one 7 x ⅜-in. (18 x 1-cm) piece of teal wool/acrylic mix felt

Fading fabric marker pen

Olive-green, dark pink, and lime-green stranded embroidery flosses (threads)

Piece of teal wool/acrylic mix felt measuring 1 in. (2.5 cm) by the circumference of your wrist plus 1¼ in. (3 cm)

Lime-green satin ribbon measuring 1 in. (2.5 cm) by the circumference of your wrist plus 2 in. (5 cm)

Lime-green sewing thread

1¼ x ¾ in. (3 x 2. cm) of hook-and-loop fastening

2 x 2 in. (5 x 5 cm) piece of thin plastic

Craft glue

Polyester fiber stuffing

Blunt-pointed knitting needle or thin chopstick

Small button

1 Using the template on page 123, cut out a circle from the pale teal felt. Using compasses, make a paper template for a circle with a 1⅛-in. (2.75-cm) radius. Use this template to cut two circles from the teal felt.

2 Using the fading fabric marker pen, copy the numbers and watch hands from the template onto the circle of pale teal felt. Using two strands of floss (thread) and a fine embroidery needle, embroider the numbers in olive-green chain stitch (see page 112) and the hands in dark pink backstitch (see page 111). Pin the embroidered circle to the center of a teal circle. Using two strands of dark pink floss, blanket stitch (see page 111) the embroidered circle in place.

3 Starting level with the embroidered number 3 and using two strands of lime-green floss (thread), blanket stitch the 7 x ⅜-in. (18 x 1-cm) strip of teal felt around the edge of the teal circle. Where the ends meet, overlap them a small amount, trim off any excess, and straight stitch (see page 111) them together.

4 Turn under ⅜ in. (1 cm) at each end of the lime-green ribbon, then pin it to the back of the felt strip that will go around your wrist. Using two strands of lime-green floss (thread), blanket stitch the ribbon to the felt along all edges.

5 Pin the plain teal circle to the center of the felt strip. Working from the ribbon side and using lime-green sewing thread and a fine sewing needle, sew a rectangle of backstitch in the center of the circle to attach it to the strap.

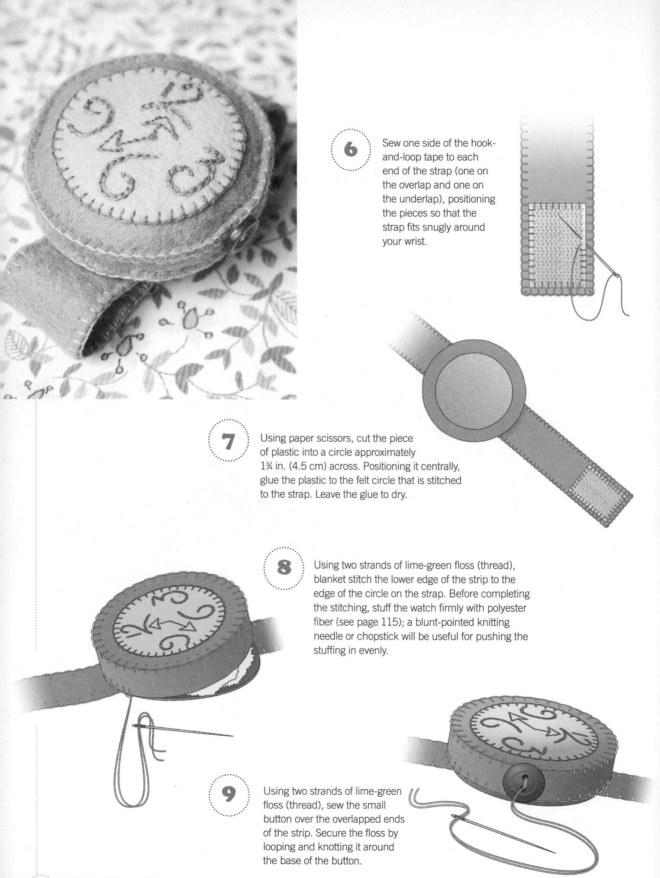

6 Sew one side of the hook-and-loop tape to each end of the strap (one on the overlap and one on the underlap), positioning the pieces so that the strap fits snugly around your wrist.

7 Using paper scissors, cut the piece of plastic into a circle approximately 1¾ in. (4.5 cm) across. Positioning it centrally, glue the plastic to the felt circle that is stitched to the strap. Leave the glue to dry.

8 Using two strands of lime-green floss (thread), blanket stitch the lower edge of the strip to the edge of the circle on the strap. Before completing the stitching, stuff the watch firmly with polyester fiber (see page 115); a blunt-pointed knitting needle or chopstick will be useful for pushing the stuffing in evenly.

9 Using two strands of lime-green floss (thread), sew the small button over the overlapped ends of the strip. Secure the floss by looping and knotting it around the base of the button.

needle-and-pin book

All stitchers need a project (or three) to take on vacation, and this is the ideal holder for the pins and needles you'll need. The bookbinder's stitch is just running stitch worked back and forth—practice on a scrap of felt before you start.

1 Fold the largest piece of felt in half widthwise and mark the center with pins. Cut three different-sized circles (they don't have to be perfectly round) from the felt scraps and arrange them on the front (the right-hand side) of the book cover, at least ⅝ in. (1.5 cm) from the pins.

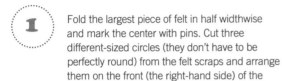

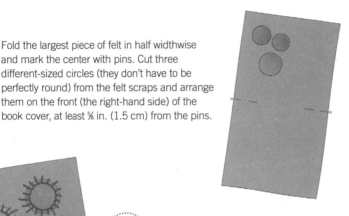

2 Using two strands of stranded floss (thread), work blanket stitch (see page 111) around the edge of each circle. Work it "inside out" so that the "legs" of the stitches extend over the edge of the circle, and make the "legs" different lengths. Blanket stitch each circle in a different color.

3 Using two strands as before, fill the center of each circle with French knots (see page 113), using all the colors. Work a few knots between the seed heads.

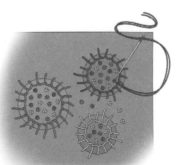

4 Using three strands of green floss (thread), work running stitch (see page 110) stems for the seed heads.

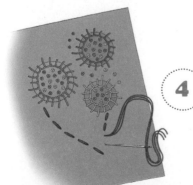

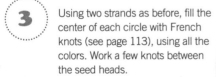

you will need

Scissors, needles, and pins

One 5 x 2¾-in. (13 x 7-cm) and three 2¾ x 2½-in. (7 x 6-cm) pieces of felt

Tiny scraps of felt in three shades of one color

Stranded embroidery flosses (threads) in three shades of one color and in green

Basting (tacking) thread

Ruler

Fading fabric marker pen

Pearl cotton embroidery floss (thread)

cutting the pages to size
If matching up all the edges in Step 5 sounds too complicated, trim the pages with pinking shears for a decorative edge and to make them smaller. Put them between the covers, positioning them evenly, and then baste (tack) the front edges together.

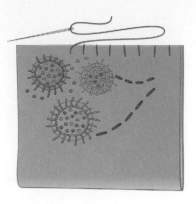

5 Slip the felt "pages" into the cover, folding it around them. Carefully match up all the visible edges, trimming a little if needed. Oversew the front edge together to baste (tack) the pages in place.

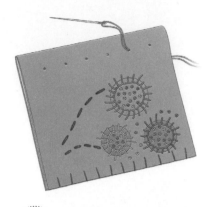

6 Using the ruler and fading fabric marker pen, mark a line of six dots $3/8$ in. (1 cm) apart on the front cover, $3/8$ in. (1 cm) from the spine of the pin book. Thread a sharp-pointed embroidery needle with a long length of pearl cotton floss (thread). Slip it between the pages and bring it out through the cover at the second mark from the top of the book. Pull the floss through, leaving a 4-in. (10-cm) tail.

7 Work running stitch along the spine, going in and out at the marked dots. Take the needle straight through the book at each dot to make the stitches as even as possible on both the front and the back. Keep turning the book over and back again to check that the stitches are even and pull them taut. Bring the needle through at the last dot, take it over the bottom edge of the book, and bring it back up where it last came out. Pull the floss (thread) taut.

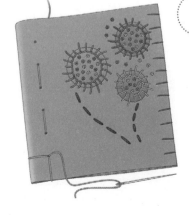

8 Take the needle over the spine of the book and bring it through again where it last came out. Pull the stitch taut.

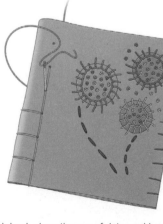

9 Work back along the row of dots, making a running stitch in each gap and then making a stitch over the spine of the book. Be careful to take the needle though a hole already stitched through each time and to pull the floss (thread) taut.

10

When you get to the other end of the book, make a stitch over the edge as in Step 7. Unpick the basting (tacking) stitches. Make a final stitch to fill in the last gap on the spine, then slip the needle between the pages to meet the tail of floss (thread) left when starting the stitching. Tie the ends together with a very firm knot.

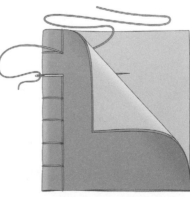

decorating the pin book

I decorated my pin book with a simple design of seed heads, but you can create whatever design you like. Embroider your name, appliqué a motif, sew on a purchased patch— the choice is yours.

fabulous finger ring

Perfect for when you are pinning alterations or dressmaking on a tailor's dummy, this pincushion will be, quite literally, on hand.

you will need

Wool roving in one or two colors

Dishwashing detergent

Warm water

Metal bottle cap

Scissors, needles, and pins

Piece of felt slightly larger than the top of the bottle cap

Fading fabric marker pen

Stranded embroidery floss (thread) to match felt

Strip of felt measuring the circumference of the bottle cap plus ¼ in. (5 mm), by about ¾ in. (2 cm)

Cutting mat

Craft knife

Piece of elastic long enough to fit loosely around forefinger, by ¼ in. (5 mm) wide

Strong sewing thread

All-purpose glue

Beading thread to match felt

Small amount of flower trim

Seed beads

1 Pull off a small piece of roving and wind it into a loose ball. Spread a little dishwashing detergent on your hands and roll the ball between your palms. Dip your hands into warm water and roll the ball more briskly and firmly. Keep dipping and rolling until the ball is firm and round. This should only take a few minutes. Wind a little more loose roving around the ball and repeat the process to make the ball larger. You can add a wind or two of a different color to create streaks on the ball. Continue until the ball is slightly larger in diameter than the metal bottle cap. Rinse the ball in cold water and leave to dry.

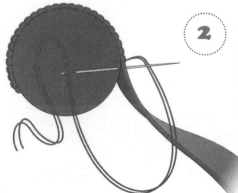

2 Lay the bottle cap on a piece of felt and draw around it using the fading fabric marker pen. Cut out the circle, cutting just outside the drawn line. Using an embroidery needle and two strands of floss (thread), blanket stitch (see page 111) the strip of felt to the edge of the circle.

3 When you have stitched right around, pop the metal cap and the ball into the felt "basket" you have made and check that the edge of the strip comes to about halfway up the felt ball. If necessary, trim the top edge of the strip a little. Then overlap the ends of the felt and sew them together with straight stitches (see page 111), using an embroidery needle and two strands of floss (thread) as before.

stuffing the pincushion

This pincushion is not stuffed as such, you simply stick your pins into the ball of wool roving (see page 115).

4 Put the felt "basket" circle-side down on the cutting mat and, using the craft knife, carefully cut two ¼-in. (5-mm) slits in the circle. Position the slits opposite each other, close to the edge of the circle. From the outside, thread an end of elastic through each slit, overlap them a little, and sew them together with strong thread. Pull the loop out at the back, so that the sewn ends stay inside the "basket," and check that the elastic fits around your finger. It needs to be tight enough to stop the ring from flopping around, but not uncomfortable.

fabulous finger ring

5 Spread some glue on the back of the bottle cap and press it down into the felt "basket." Leave to dry.

6 Spread some glue inside the metal cap and put the ball into it. Leave to dry.

7 Thread a beading needle with a long length of beading thread. Push the needle right through the ball, level with the top edge of the felt. Make a small stitch into the felt, then push the needle through the ball again. Continue in this way until the felt is stitched to the ball all around.

8 Pin the trim around the pincushion, covering the join between the felt and the ball. Using a sewing needle and beading thread, sew the trim to the ball with small stitches.

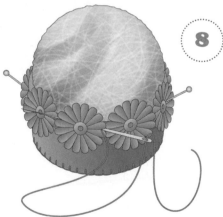

9 Using a beading needle and beading thread, sew a seed bead into the center of each flower in the trim.

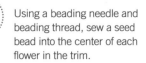

pincushion with pockets

The little pockets right around the edge of this pincushion are perfect for holding the bits and pieces you are using while sewing a particular project. Spools of thread, scissors, thimble, buttons, marker pen...there's a home for all of these and more.

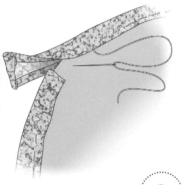

1 Using the iron, press the binding in half lengthwise. Fold it over the edge of one of the fabric circles, and baste (tack) it in place right around the circle. When you get to the starting point, cut off the excess leaving a ¾-in. (2-cm) overlap. Fold the end under by ⅜ in. (1 cm) to neaten it, and baste (tack) it over the starting end.

2 Set the sewing machine to a narrow zigzag stitch and thread it with sewing thread to match the binding. Sew the binding to the fabric right around the circle, stitching on the binding, very close to the inner edge. Repeat Steps 1 and 2 with the second fabric circle.

you will need

- 2yd (1.8 m) of bias binding
- Iron
- Two circles of cotton fabric with a radius of 5 in. (13 cm)
- Scissors, needles, and pins
- Basting (tacking) thread
- Sewing machine
- Sewing threads to match fabric and binding
- Compasses
- Fading fabric marker pen
- Polyester fiber stuffing
- Pearl cotton embroidery floss (thread)
- ¾-in. (2-cm) self-cover button
- Small two-hole button

3 Using compasses and the fading fabric marker pen, draw an inner circle with a radius of 2⅞ in. (7.5 cm) on the right side of one circle of fabric. Set the sewing machine to a small straight stitch and thread it with thread to match the fabric. Pin the two circles wrong sides together and sew around the marked inner circle, leaving a gap for stuffing. Fill the pincushion with polyester fiber, stuffing it quite firmly, then backstitch (see page 111) the gap closed.

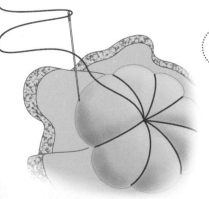

4 Thread a doll needle with a length of pearl cotton floss (thread)—a length four times the circumference of the stuffed pincushion will be ample. Starting on the bottom, use the cotton to divide the pincushion up in the same way as for the Pumpkin Patch pincushion (see page 92)—but instead of taking the needle right around the edge of the pincushion, take it around the edge of the stuffed section only, pushing the needle through the fabric just inside the inner line of stitching. You will have a divided pincushion surrounded by a ring of two layers of fabric.

5 Using the fading fabric marker pen, make a mark on the outer edge of the ring of fabric, just inside the binding, in line with each division line on the stuffed section.

6 Thread the doll needle with another length of pearl cotton floss (thread) and bring the needle up through the middle of the pincushion from bottom to top.

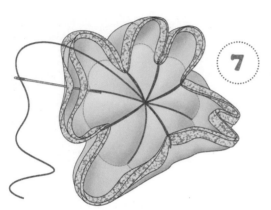

7 Take the needle over the edge of the ring of fabric and, from the underside, put it through both layers at a marked point. Then push the needle into the stuffed section of the pincushion, on the division line that matches the marked point and ⅝ in. (1.5 cm) inside the inner line of stitching between the stuffed and flat sections. Push the needle through the pincushion at an angle, so that it comes out in the middle of the base, where all the other division threads come out, and pull tight. Repeat to catch every marked point up against a division line.

8 Iron the remaining binding flat and use a bit of it to cover the button, following the manufacturer's instructions. Thread the doll needle with a length of pearl cotton and double it. Take the needle up through the pincushion from bottom to top and thread on the covered button. Take the needle back down through the middle of the pincushion, but do not pull the floss (thread) tight.

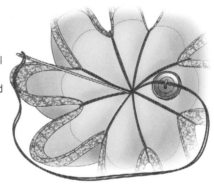

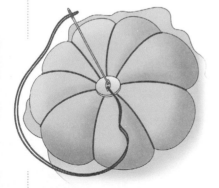

9 Thread on the small button, then take the needle back up through the pincushion and through the shank of the covered button, and back down through the pincushion again. Take it out through the button, then slowly and firmly pull the floss (thread) very tight. Take the needle through the bottom button and out to one side and secure the floss by looping and knotting it around under the button.

for your sewing machine

This pincushion is a kind of padded "belt" that you can fasten around the front of your sewing machine. It's so quick and easy to make and so practical to use when you are machining that you'll wonder how you ever got by without it.

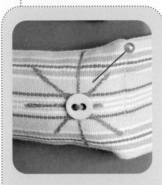

you will need

Tape measure

Two pieces of sturdy fabric
(see Step 1 for size)

Scissors, needles, and pins

Machine embroidery threads
(optional)

Decorative button (optional)

Sewing machine

Sewing thread to match fabric

Polyester fiber stuffing

Ruler

Basting (tacking) thread

Two snap fasteners

 1 Measure the circumference of the upright part of your sewing machine and add 3 in. (8 cm). Work out how deep the pincushion can be without interfering with the machine's functions and add 1¼ in. (3 cm). Cut two pieces of fabric to these measurements.

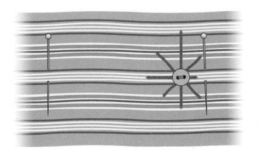

 2 Fold one strip in half lengthwise and mark the middle with a pin. Measure the width of the front of the upright part of your machine. Using pins, mark this width on the fabric band, centering it on the midpoint pin, which you then remove. The marked area will be the pincushion itself and you can embroider this area—or not—as you wish. Keep the stitches at least ⅝ in. (1.5 cm) from the top and bottom edges. I machine-embroidered a simple star in two types of pink thread and stitched a vintage linen button into the center of it.

 3 Remove the marker pins, then pin the two pieces right sides together, matching all raw edges. Set the sewing machine to a medium straight stitch. Taking a ⅝-in. (1.5-cm) seam allowance, sew along one long edge, across a short end, and back along the other long edge. Turn right side out and press. Turn in ⅝ in. (1.5 cm) on the open short end and press.

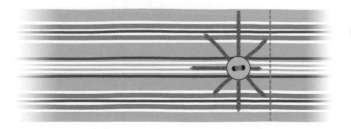

 4 Using pins, mark out the pincushion section as in Step 2. Using matching thread, machine-sew a line across the band at the marked point furthest from the open end of the band. Secure the threads firmly on the back of the band.

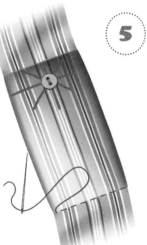

5 Reposition the pin marking the other end of the pincushion section so that it is only in the front piece of fabric. Push polyester stuffing down the band, using a ruler to push it along, to fill the pincushion section of the band (between the stitched line and the remaining pin). Pack the stuffing in as tightly as possible. Replace the pin through both layers, then baste (tack) along the pin line.

stuffing the pincushion
This pincushion is firmly stuffed with polyester fiber to make it plump, but also keep it as lightweight as possible (see page 115).

6 Fit a zipper foot to the sewing machine and sew along the basting (tacking) line. Secure the threads on the back, as before. Sew across the open end of the band. Remove the basting stitches.

7 Using doubled thread, sew snaps to each end of the band, positioning them so that the band fits tightly around the upright part of the sewing machine.

for your sewing machine

a great **gift**

This is a really useful pincushion, as well as being very pretty. It's magnetic, so pins just leap toward it, and it has a carborundum grit filling so you can push pins into it to sharpen them. It may look like a gift, but you won't want to give it away!

you will need

Iron

Two 2½ x 2½-in. (6 x 6-cm) and one 10 x ¾-in. (25 x 2-cm) pieces of medium-weight iron-on interfacing

Two 2½ x 2½-in. (6 x 6-cm) and one 10 x ¾-in. (25 x 2-cm) pieces of wool/acrylic mix felt

16 in. (40 cm) ribbon, ¾ in. (2 cm) wide

Scissors, needles, and pins

Sewing threads to match felt and ribbon

All-purpose glue

Flat ¾ x 1-in. (2 x 2.5-cm) magnet

Carborundum grit

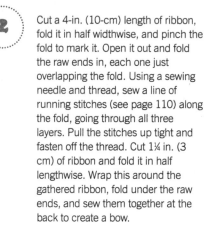

1 Iron the pieces of interfacing onto the back of the pieces of felt. Using scissors, round off the corners of the felt squares. Using a sewing needle and matching sewing thread, blanket stitch (see page 111) the strip to one of the squares. Start in the middle of one side, leaving ⅜ in. (1 cm) loose, and stitch right around. When you reach the beginning of the strip, overlap the ends (trimming off any excess felt if need be) and sew them together with straight stitches (see page 111).

2 Cut a 4-in. (10-cm) length of ribbon, fold it in half widthwise, and pinch the fold to mark it. Open it out and fold the raw ends in, each one just overlapping the fold. Using a sewing needle and thread, sew a line of running stitches (see page 110) along the fold, going through all three layers. Pull the stitches up tight and fasten off the thread. Cut 1¼ in. (3 cm) of ribbon and fold it in half lengthwise. Wrap this around the gathered ribbon, fold under the raw ends, and sew them together at the back to create a bow.

cutting out pieces

You may find it easier to iron a large piece of interfacing onto a large piece of felt, then cut out the individual pieces.

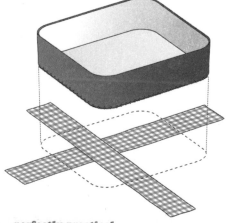

3 Cut the remaining ribbon in half and lay it flat in the shape of a cross. Lay the pincushion right side down on top of the ribbon, positioning it so that the cross is close to one corner. Fold the ends of the ribbon over the edges of the side strip and glue them to the inside of the pincushion. Make sure that the ribbon is not too tight or it will pull in the sides.

4 Using a sewing needle and matching thread, sew the bow that you made in Step 2 to the ribbon cross on top of the pincushion, stitching through the back of the central wrapping strip.

5 Glue the magnet into the inside of the pincushion, positioning it in the opposite corner to the bow. Leave the glue to dry.

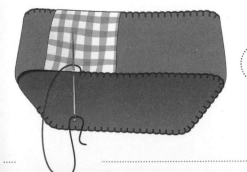

6 Using a sewing needle and matching thread, blanket stitch the remaining square of felt to the free edge of the strip. Before completing the stitching, fill the pincushion with carborundum grit (see page 115), then finish the blanket stitching.

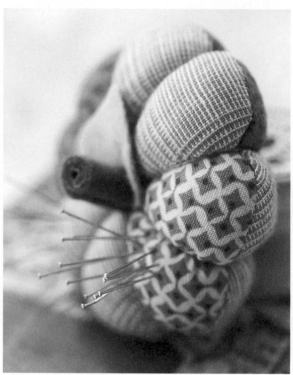

good enough **to eat**

Doughnut pincushion ✳ Pumpkin patch ✳ Toadstool pincushion
Slice of cake ✳ Summer strawberry ✳ The perfect pear
Peas in a pod

doughnut pincushion

As sweet as sugar, this little doughnut is delightful I've chosen pink "frosting" and silver "sprinkles," but you can use whichever colors make your mouth water the most.

1 Using compasses, draw on paper a circle with a 2-in. (5-cm) radius. Placing the point of the compasses in the same spot, draw an inner circle with a ⅝-in. (1.5-cm) radius to create a doughnut-shaped template. Cut two doughnuts from brown felt. Using the frosting template on page 123, cut one frosting shape from sugar-pink felt.

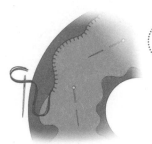

2 Pin the frosting to one of the brown doughnuts, positioning it centrally. Using three strands of embroidery floss (thread) and a fine embroidery needle, blanket stitch (see page 111) around the inner and outer edges of the frosting.

3 Using the beading thread and a beading needle, sew bugle and seed bead "sprinkles" onto the frosting, positioning them in random clusters for best effect.

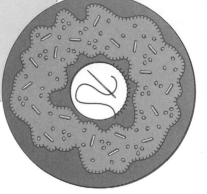

4 Wrong sides together, pin the decorated top to the remaining brown doughnut. Using a sewing needle and brown sewing thread, sew them together with a small, tight blanket stitch around the inner circle.

5 Sew the outer edges together in the same way, stuffing the doughnut with polyester fiber as you go (see page 115). Sew a short section, then stuff it to ensure that the doughnut is evenly filled.

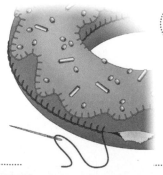

stuffing the pincushion

This pincushion is stuffed with polyester fiber to make it spongy and lightweight. You could use either kapok or wool roving if you prefer (see page 115).

variation

This giant doughnut is a super-handy sewing-tool
carrier as well as a pincushion. It has an outer radius of
3 in. (8 cm) and an inner radius of 1⅜ in. (3.5 cm) and is
made in the same way as the little doughnut, but with
orange frosting and pink and orange sprinkles. Once it
is stuffed, lay it face down and pin a 4⅝-in. (11.5-cm)
circle of felt over the central hole. Using sewing thread
and blanket stitch, sew this circle to the doughnut.

pumpkin **patch**

This pincushion is styled to look like a plump pumpkin. Choose a variety of print fabrics—I used three fabrics, but you could also use two or four different patterns.

1 Using compasses, draw on paper a circle with a 2½-in. (6-cm) radius. Using this as a template, cut a circle from each piece of printed fabric. Fold each circle in half and press it, then cut along the pressed line. Fold each semicircle in half, press, and cut along the line so that each circle of fabric is divided into even quarters. Do this accurately, as it'll help later if the pieces are all the same size.

you will need

Compasses

Paper for template

Scissors, needles, and pins

Fading fabric marker pen

2¾ x 2¾-in. (7 x 7-cm) pieces of printed cotton fabric

Sewing machine

Sewing threads to match cotton fabrics and brown felt

Iron

Polyester fiber stuffing

Blunt-pointed knitting needle or thin chopstick

Pearl cotton embroidery floss (thread)

Fabric glue

1¼ x 1⅜-in. (3 x 3.5-cm) piece of brown felt

Sticky tape

Leaf template (page 123)

1¼ x 1¼-in. (3 x 3-cm) piece of green felt

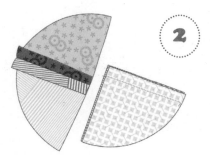

2 Set the sewing machine to a small straight stitch. Pin two differently patterned quarters right sides together. Taking a ⅜-in. (1-cm) seam allowance, sew along one straight edge. Press the seam open. Repeat to make four semicircles.

3 Pin the semicircles right sides together and sew them as before to make two complete circles. Pin the two circles right sides together, aligning differently patterned quarters and carefully matching the seams.

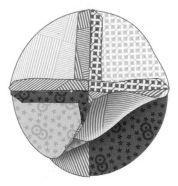

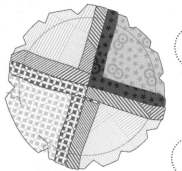

4 Taking a ⅜-in. (1-cm) seam allowance, machine-sew around the edge of the circle, leaving a small gap for turning through. Clip notches in the seam allowance all around the stitched section (see page 116).

5 Turn the pincushion right side out. Do not press the seam, but do press under the edges of the gap. Stuff the pincushion with polyester fiber (see page 115), making it well filled but not firm. Ladder stitch the gap closed (see page 111).

Cut a long length of pearl cotton floss (thread) about four times the circumference of the fabric ball and thread a long needle; a doll needle is ideal, although a long darner will work, too. Tie a big knot in the floss 4 in. (10 cm) from the end. Push the needle right through the center of the pincushion, going in and emerging at the meeting point of the four quarters. Pull the floss (thread) through to the knot.

 Pass the needle around the outside of the pincushion, over the seam between two adjoining patches of fabric, and then take it back up through the center of the pincushion in the same place as before. Pull the floss (thread) as tight as possible. Repeat the process on the opposite side of the pincushion and then at the two remaining compass points to divide the pincushion into four segments, each defined by a tight line of floss.

 Repeat the process to divide each segment in half to create a total of eight segments. Take a stitch back down through the pincushion and tie the end of the floss (thread) to the starting tail with a very firm knot.

even segments Pull the floss (thread) equally tight each time to make the segments as even as possible.

 Spread fabric glue thinly on one side of the piece of brown felt and roll it up as tightly as possible. Use a piece of sticky tape to hold the roll while the glue dries. Once it is dry, use scissors to trim the top and bottom of the stalk to make them flat and even.

 Using the leaf template on page 123, cut a leaf from the green felt.

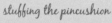 Position the leaf on top of the pumpkin and stand the stalk on top of that. Using brown sewing thread and tiny stitches, sew the end of the stalk to the pumpkin, sewing through the leaf to catch it in place.

stuffing the pincushion

This pincushion is stuffed with polyester fiber as it needs to be very spongy so that it can be pulled in by the pearl cotton floss (thread) (see page 115). Pulling the segments of the pincushion in makes it very firm.

toadstool pincushion

Whoever would have thought a toadstool could be cute?
This one certainly is! Copy the face shown here or create your
own features to give your pincushion personality.

1 Using the templates on page 123, cut four top caps and one bottom cap from red felt. From white felt, cut two stalks and one bottom cap, cutting around the outer edge only to make a circle. Use the compasses to draw a circle with a radius of ⅞ in. (2.25 cm) on white felt and cut it out. Cut one tiny circle and one larger circle from turquoise felt for eyes. Cut nine small circles of varying sizes from white felt.

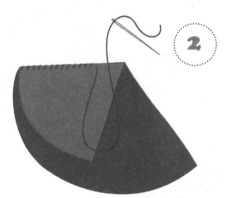

2 Right sides together and using red sewing thread, a fine sewing needle, and whip stitch (see page 111), sew the top cap pieces together along the straight edges. Turn the cap right side out.

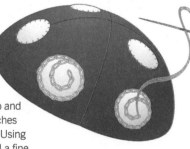

3 Arrange the white circles on the top cap and sew them in place with tiny straight stitches (see page 111) in white sewing thread. Using three strands of white floss (thread) and a fine embroidery needle, sew around the outer edge of each circle with chain stitch (see page 112), continuing the stitching onto the circle itself to make a small spiral.

4 Using red sewing thread and tiny running stitches (see page 110), sew the red bottom cap to the white bottom cap along the wavy inner edge. Trim the white felt along the outer edge to ⅛ in. (2 mm) inside the red felt.

you will need

Toadstool templates (page 123)

Fading fabric marker pen

Four 2½ x 2½-in. (6 x 6-cm) and one 3¼ x 3¼-in. (8.5 x 8.5-cm) piece of red wool/acrylic mix felt

Scissors, needles, and pins

Two 2⅞ x 1¾-in. (7.5 x 4.5-cm), one 3¼ x 3¼-in. (8.5 x 8.5-cm), and one 2 x 2-in. (5 x 5-cm) piece of white wool/acrylic mix felt

Compasses

Scrap of turquoise felt

Red, white, turquoise, and black sewing threads

White and red stranded embroidery flosses (threads)

Two tiny black seed beads

5 x 5-in. (12 x 12-cm) piece of cotton fabric

Sand

Polyester fiber stuffing

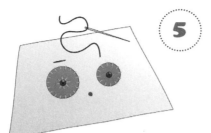

5 Using turquoise sewing thread and straight stitch, sew the eyes to one of the stalk pieces. Sew a straight-stitch star in turquoise in the center of the larger eye. Using black thread and a beading needle if necessary, sew a bead in the center of each eye, sewing them on flat like an "O." Make a little straight stitch in black above each eye for an eyebrow and a tiny red French knot (see page 113) for a nose.

6 Wrong sides together and using three strands of white floss (thread) and blanket stitch (see page 111), sew the stalk pieces together down the sides. Gently squash the seams to make the stalk as circular as possible and pin it to the center of the bottom cap. Using three strands of white floss and straight stitch, sew the stalk to the bottom cap.

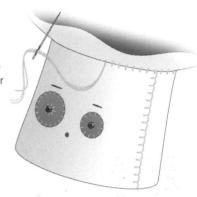

7 Use the compasses to draw a circle with a 2½-in. (6-cm) radius on the cotton fabric. Cut it out and turn under a narrow hem all around. Using doubled white sewing thread, work small running stitches all around the hem. Pull up the stitches until there is just a small opening and fill the bag with sand. Pull the stitches tight and secure the thread with several stitches over the gathers.

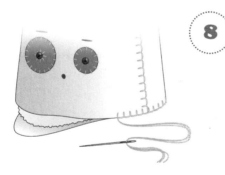

8 Stuff the top of the stalk with polyester stuffing (see page 115), then push the sandbag in, gathered side first. Pin the white circle to the base of the stalk and sew it in place with three strands of white floss (thread) and blanket stitch, pushing in more polyester stuffing as you go so that the stalk is evenly filled.

9 Pin the top cap to the bottom cap around the edges. Using three strands of red floss (thread) and blanket stitch, sew the top to the bottom. Before you complete the stitching, stuff the cap with polyester fiber—don't pack it in firmly—then finish the stitching. Press the cap down on one side to position it at a jaunty angle.

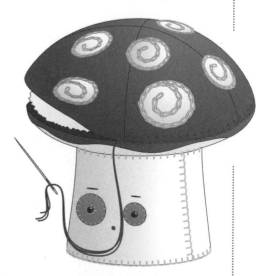

stuffing the pincushion

This pincushion is mainly stuffed with polyester fiber (see page 115) to keep the cap of the toadstool as lightweight as possible. The stalk has a bag of sand inside it to weight the pincushion down.

slice of cake

This is a slice of sponge cake with raspberry jam filling and pink frosting. You could choose deep brown needlecord and yellow patterned fabric for a chocolate sponge with lemon frosting; or whatever colors work best for your favorite cake.

you will need

One 14 x 2¾-in. (35 x 7-cm), one 5½ x 5½ -in. (14 x 14-cm), one 5½ x 3¾-in. (14 x 9.5-cm), and one 9½ x 1¼-in. (24 x 3-cm) piece of patterned cotton fabric

Scissors, needles, and pins

Iron

Basting (tacking) thread

Cake template (page 124)

Fading fabric marker pen

Sewing machine

Sewing threads to match fabrics and rick-rack

9½ x 4¼-in. (24 x 10.5-cm) piece of needlecord fabric

10¼ in. (26 cm) of jumbo rick-rack

Three 5½ x 5½-in. (14 x 14-cm) pieces of felt

Polyester fiber stuffing

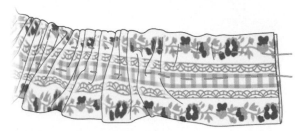

1 Turn under the short ends of the 14 x 2¾-in. (35 x 7-cm) piece of fabric by ¾ in. (2 cm) and press them. Fold the strip in half lengthwise and press it. Using basting (tacking) thread, work two lines of running stitches (see page 110) along it, one line ¼ in. (5 mm) up from the open long edge and one a further ⅜ in. (1 cm) up from the first line. Pull the threads up to make a ruffle that is 4⅛ in. (10.5 cm) long. Knot the threads together.

2 Using the template on page 124, cut the shape out from the square piece of cotton fabric. Right sides together, pin the raw edges of the ruffle to the curved edge of the cake top, positioning it centrally. Set the sewing machine to a medium straight stitch and, taking a ⅜ in. (1 cm) seam allowance, sew the ruffle to the cake top. Take out the gathering stitches.

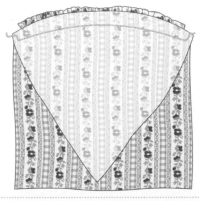

3 Right sides together, pin the curved edge of the cake top to the 5½ x 3¾-in. (14 x 9.5-cm) piece of cotton fabric (the back piece), so that the ruffle is trapped between the layers. Set the sewing machine to a small straight stitch and machine-sew the pieces together.

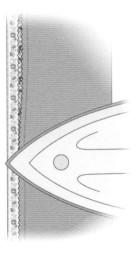

stuffing the pincushion

This pincushion is stuffed with polyester fiber to fill it out without distorting the shape (see page 115).

4 Right sides together, sew the last piece of cotton fabric to one long edge of the needlecord fabric. Open out and press the fabric, pressing the seam upward. (This piece is referred to as the sides piece from now on.)

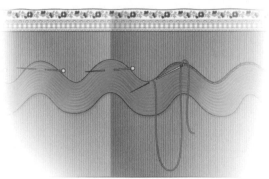

5 Pin the rick-rack to the sides piece, with the top of the scallops ¾ in. (2 cm) from the seam between the needlecord and the cotton. Sew the rick-rack in place with short backstitches (see page 111) along both edges. Wrong sides together, fold the sides piece in half widthwise and press the fold, then open it out again.

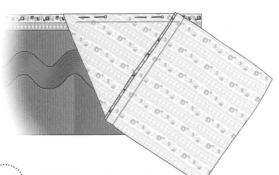

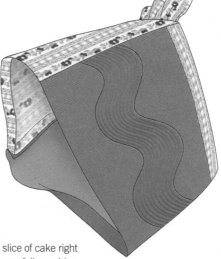

6 Right sides together, match the point of the cake top to the pressed fold in the sides piece. Pin and then machine-sew the pieces together along one straight edge of the top.

7 Go back to the point of the cake top and pin then sew the other end of the sides piece to the other side of the top. You'll need to clip into the seam allowance at the top of the sides piece to do this.

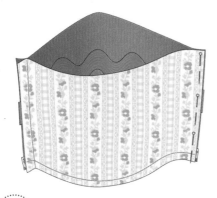

8 Right sides together, pin the ends of the sides piece to the edges of the cotton back piece. Machine-sew both seams.

9 Turn the slice of cake right side out, carefully pushing out all the corners and points. Press under a ⅜-in. (1-cm) hem all around the lower edge.

10 Cut the template along the dotted line and cut three shapes from felt. Holding two together to form a double layer, slip these into the top of the cake, tucking the edges under the seam allowances. Fit the third piece into the bottom of the cake and pin it in place. Using matching sewing thread and blanket stitch (see page 111), sew the base in place, leaving a small gap for stuffing. Fill the cake with polyester fiber, being careful not to overfill it and so distort the shape, then complete the stitching.

summer **strawberry**

This traditional pincushion is filled with carborundum grit to keep your pins and needles bright and sharp, and has a rick-rack trim to add a fresh twist.

you will need

Strawberry template (page 124)

Scissors, needles, and pins

Fading fabric marker pen

Two 4½ x 4-in. (11 x 10-cm) pieces of pink velvet

Sewing machine

Sewing threads to match fabric and felt

Pinking shears

Blunt-pointed knitting needle or thin chopstick

Beading thread to match fabric

Shot glass or small cup

Carborundum grit

Kapok stuffing

14 in. (35 cm) green rick-rack

Compasses

2 x 2-in. (5 x 5-cm) piece of green felt

Green seed beads

Fray check

 Using the template on page 124, cut two strawberry shapes from velvet. Pin the pieces right sides together. Set the sewing machine to a medium straight stitch. Setting the edge of the presser foot against the edge of the fabric, sew around the curved edges of the strawberry, leaving the straight top edge open. Trim the seam allowances with pinking shears.

 Turn the strawberry right side out, carefully poking out the point with a blunt-tipped knitting needle or a thin chopstick. Thread a sewing needle with beading thread (for strength), double it, and knot the ends, leaving a short tail. Starting and finishing on the right side, work running stitch (see page 110) around the top of the strawberry, not too close to the edge of the fabric.

3 Stand the strawberry in a shot glass or small cup and fill it with carborundum grit. Shake it down as much as possible to make the strawberry very firm. Fill it to about ⅜ in. (1 cm) below the stitching, then pack kapok into the top.

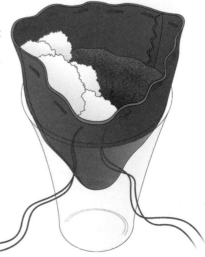

4

Pull on the threads to gather the top of the strawberry over the kapok. Before tightening it completely, push in as much kapok as you can to make the strawberry as firm as possible. Tighten the gathers and knot the ends of the threads firmly.

stuffing the pincushion

This pincushion is stuffed primarily with carborundum grit, with just a little kapok in the hull end (see page 115).

5 Cut a 3-in. (8-cm) length of rick-rack. Fold it in half and, using green sewing thread, sew the loop together about ⅜ in. (1 cm) from the ends. Splay the ends out across the top of the gathers in the strawberry and sew them in place.

Sewing on beads Strawberry seeds don't appear in any particular pattern, so just sew on beads to suit you. Don't sew on too many or they'll get in the way of the pins.

6 Cut a circle 1¾ in. (4.5 cm) in diameter from the green felt. Cut a tiny slit in the middle of the circle. Slip the slit over the loop of rick-rack so that the felt covers the gathered end of the strawberry. Using green sewing thread and tiny straight stitches (see page 111), sew the felt in place. You'll need to make a few small tucks in the edge to make the circle sit neatly over the top of the strawberry.

7 Thread a beading needle with beading thread to match the fabric. Secure the thread under the edge of the felt circle. Take the needle through the strawberry and thread on a green seed bead. Take the needle back through the strawberry close to where it came out, and bring it out again where you want the next bead. Pull the thread as tight as possible and repeat until the strawberry is beaded to your satisfaction. Take the needle back up to the top and secure it under the felt again.

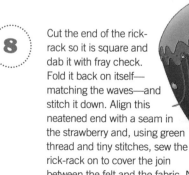

8 Cut the end of the rick-rack so it is square and dab it with fray check. Fold it back on itself—matching the waves—and stitch it down. Align this neatened end with a seam in the strawberry and, using green thread and tiny stitches, sew the rick-rack on to cover the join between the felt and the fabric. Neaten the other end in the same way as the first to finish it. Sew on another length halfway up the green felt hull.

the perfect pear

An elegant pincushion that'll look beautiful sitting on your work table. If you really love it, make a huge one and fill it with sand to act as a doorstop.

 Using the template on page 125, draw around the pear piece onto the fabric and cut out six shapes. You can use different fabrics or the same one; I used the same one but turned it for three of the shapes so that the pattern ran at 90 degrees. Draw around the leaf template onto felt and cut out one shape.

 Pin two pear pieces right sides together. Set the sewing machine to a medium straight stitch and, taking a ⅜-in. (1-cm) seam allowance, sew down one side from top to bottom, reversing at each end to secure the stitching.

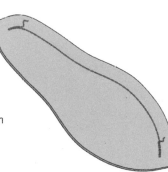

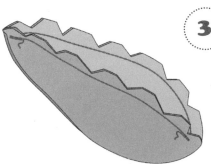

3 Right sides together, pin a third pear piece to the open side of one of the first two. Sew a side seam as before. Notch all the seams around the curves (see page 116). Sew the other three pieces together in the same way to produce two pear halves.

 Pin the two halves right sides together. Sew up one seam as before, and sew the other one from the base to about two-thirds of the way to the top. Notch the curves and turn right side out. Press under the seam allowances along the gap.

you will need

Pear templates (page 125)

Scissors, needles, and pins

Fading fabric marker pen

Six 6¼ x 2¾-in. (16 x 7-cm) pieces of cotton fabric

One 4 x 2-in. (10 x 5-cm) piece of felt

Sewing machine

Sewing thread to match fabric

Polyester fiber stuffing

Fine sand

Small twig

Stranded embroidery floss (thread) to match felt

stuffing the pincushion

This pincushion is stuffed with polyester fiber, with some sand spooned in to give it weight. You could stuff it with kapok or wool roving if you prefer (see page 115).

5 Stuff the base of the pear with polyester fiber to fill it out, then spoon in about six tablespoons of sand to add weight. Fill the top of the pear with polyester fiber, slip stitching (see page 111) the gap closed as you do so. At the top, slip one end of the twig into the opening, then finish stitching. Take the needle through the fabric around the base of the pear and pull it tight to hold the twig in place.

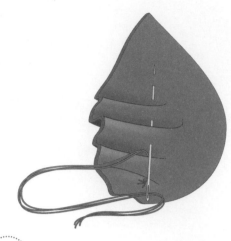

6 Thread an embroidery needle with three strands of floss (thread). Work a line of running stitches (see page 110) down the felt leaf, positioning the line off center and starting and finishing on the wrong side. Pull the floss (thread) tight to ruche the felt up a bit and fasten it off.

making a stalk If you prefer, you can give your pear a rolled felt stalk, like the one in Pumpkin Patch (see page 92).

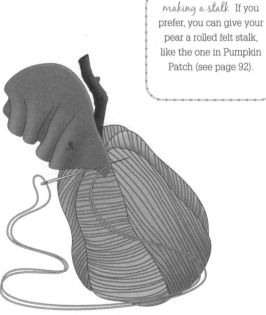

7 Folding the leaf back on itself, sew the tip of the right side to the top of the pear using doubled sewing thread. Fold the leaf down so the right side faces out and catch it in place with a couple of stitches through the floss (thread) running stitches on the back.

peas in a pod

Certainly good enough to consider nibbling on, this cute pea pod also makes a great home for pins and needles.

1 Pull off a small piece of roving and wind it into a loose ball. Spread a little dishwashing detergent on your hands and roll the ball between your palms. Dip your hands into warm water and roll the ball more briskly and firmly. Keep dipping and rolling until the ball is firm and round. This should only take a few minutes. You'll need to experiment with sizes, but you want three balls about ⅝ in. (1.5 cm) across and two balls about ⅜ in. (1 cm) across. Rinse the balls in cold water and leave to dry.

2 Sandwich the two smaller pieces of felt together with the fusible bonding web to make one double-thickness piece. Press carefully, ensuring the pieces are firmly bonded. Using the templates on page by 125, cut one base from the double-thickness felt and two side pieces from the other pieces of felt.

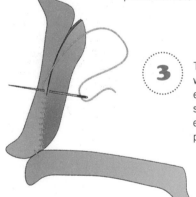

3 Thread a fine embroidery needle with the woolen thread. Join the two side pieces at one end of the straight edges with a single straight stitch. Fit the base piece against the straight edge of one side piece and blanket stitch (see page 111) the two pieces together.

4 Continue blanket stitching to join the other side piece to the base. You may find it useful to push pins through the side of the pod into the base to hold the pieces in position while you stitch—but take care not to stab yourself on the pin points. Do not fasten off the thread.

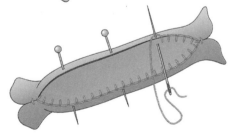

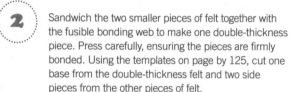

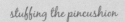

stuffing the pincushion

This pincushion is not stuffed as such,
you simply stick your pins into the peas made
from wool roving (see page 115).

5 Spread a little glue onto the underside of each pea and arrange them in the pod. The small peas sit at each end. Leave the glue to dry.

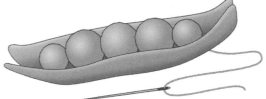

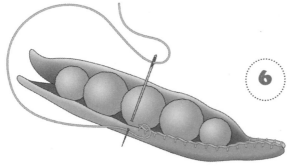

6 Continue blanket stitching to join the ends of the two side pieces together, then stitch along one side of the pod. As you reach each pea, make a couple of blanket stitches through it to sew it to the pod. Blanket stitch the other ends of the pod together and finish by stitching along the other side, stitching into the peas as before.

techniques

transferring designs onto fabric

Pages 117–125 contain the templates for the pincushions in this book, and you'll need to transfer them onto the fabric if you want to copy the design exactly.

If you only need the outline of a shape, then just photocopy the template (all the templates are shown at 100 percent and do not have to be enlarged), and cut it out. Lay it on or pin it to the fabric (whichever suits you), draw around it with a fading fabric marker pen (don't be tempted to use an ordinary pen or pencil, as they can permanently mark and spoil your project), and then cut out the shape.

If you need to transfer marks that are on the template, such as the facial features for the Matryoshka Dolls on page 34, then there are various ways of doing this and various pieces of equipment that you can buy to implement them. However, I use a simple variation on a very traditional technique and find it works well. Using a fairly thick, sharp needle (such as a crewel needle), prick holes at intervals along the line you want to copy. Make sure you prick holes at the very ends of lines and at any corners. Lay the template on the fabric, draw around the outside edge, then firmly press the fabric marker over the holes you have pricked. Lift the template off and there should be a series of small dots that you can join dot-to-dot style to produce the markings that you need.

practical stitches

These are the stitches you'll need to actually assemble the pincushions. Some of them are decorative as well, so you get a pretty and practical result.

RUNNING STITCH
The simplest stitch there is, but it never loses its charm.

Bring the needle up at A, down at B, and up at C. Repeat, bringing the needle up and back down through the fabric several times along the stitching line. Try to space the stitches evenly and make them all the same length.

WHIPPED RUNNING STITCH
A pretty variation on the simplest stitch.

Work a line of running stitch (see left). Using a blunt needle and a contrasting color of thread, bring the needle to the right side at the start of the line, then slide it under each stitch from top to bottom, without piercing the fabric, and pull it through gently.

STRAIGHT STITCH

These tiny stitches are perfect for attaching felt appliqués.

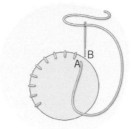

Work very short stitches just over the edge of the piece being appliquéd, bring the needle up at A, down at B, and so on around the shape.

BACKSTITCH

The ultimate utility stitch before the sewing machine was invented.

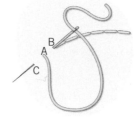

Working from right to left, bring the needle up at A, down at B, and up at C, one stitch length ahead of A.

BLANKET STITCH

This is my favorite hand-seaming stitch. It's quick to work, looks great, and makes a firm seam.

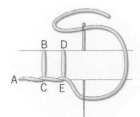

Bring the needle up at A, down at B, and up at C (directly below B), looping the thread under the needle tip. Pull the needle through, then insert it at D and bring it out at E, again looping the thread under the tip.

If you are joining two pieces of fabric, the principle is the same, but the horizontal bar of thread lies along the edge of the fabric, as shown on the right.

WHIP STITCH

This quick-to-work utility stitch is used to join fabrics either right sides or wrong sides together.

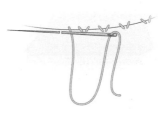

Hold together the fabrics that are being joined. From the back, take the needle through both layers, close to the edge. Repeat, taking the needle to the back and through both layers again a short distance further along. Pull through to complete the stitch. Take care not to loop the thread under the needle tip, otherwise you'll end up working blanket stitch. If you are joining the fabrics wrong sides together, you can hide the starting knot between the layers.

LADDER STITCH

This is the best stitch for closing up the final gap in a machine- or hand-sewn seam once the project has been turned right side out.

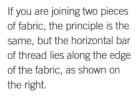

Turn in the seam allowances across the gap and press them with your fingers. Bring the needle up through the pressed fold at A, then take it straight across the gap to B. Make a tiny stitch through the folded edge and bring it back to the front at C.

SLIP STITCH

This stitch is used to attach hemmed fabric appliqués.

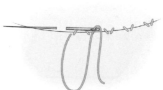

Make a tiny stitch through the base fabric, then slide the needle through the folded edge of the piece being appliquéd for about ¼ in. (5 mm).

decorative stitches

These are the lovely—but not difficult to work—embroidery stitches used on some of the projects. If you've not worked a stitch before, do practice on a scrap of fabric before starting a project.

BEADED BLANKET STITCH

This is both a decorative edging stitch and a practical joining stitch. It's surprisingly quick and easy to work.

Work as for blanket stitch (see page 111), but before you take the needle through the fabric, thread on a bead. Slide the bead down to sit close to the last stitch made. Make the smallest possible stitch through the fabric. Loop the working thread under the tip of the needle—making sure the bead doesn't follow it—and pull the thread taut so that the bead sits on the edge of the fabric.

DOUBLE BEADED BLANKET STITCH

A version of beaded blanket stitch that produces a more ornate edge.

Work as for beaded blanket stitch (see left), but you must take the needle through the fabric from front to back. Before taking the needle through, thread on two beads. Take a stitch at least the length of the bead through the fabric and pull the thread through to make a small loop. Take the needle through the loop, making sure there is a bead on either side of it. Pull the thread taut and one bead will sit on the edge of the fabric and the other on the "leg" of the stitch.

BARGELLO STITCH

This is just a simple straight canvas stitch, so easy to work. Start in the center of the canvas and work outward to the left; then return to the center and work outward to the right. This first row sets the pattern for the rest of the work,

Work a line of stepped straight stitches, bringing the needle up at A, down at B, up at C, down at D, and so on, keeping them all the same length.

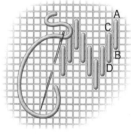

Work subsequent rows above and below the center row in the same way.

CHAIN STITCH

This is both easy to work and forgiving of inexperience, so ideal for novice embroiderers.

Bring the needle up at A, then loop the thread and insert the needle at A again. Bring it up at B, looping the thread under the needle tip. Pull the thread through.

Insert the needle at B and bring it up at C, again looping the thread under the needle tip. Continue, keeping all the stitches the same length. To anchor the last stitch in the chain, take the needle down just outside the loop, forming a little bar or "tie."

DETACHED CHAIN STITCH

Single loops that can be worked in groups to make great daisy flowers.

Work as for chain stitch (see opposite), bringing the needle up inside the loop. To finish off the stitch, take the needle down just outside the loop, forming a little bar or "tie."

OPEN CRETAN STITCH

This stitch looks more complex than it is to work, so don't be put off.

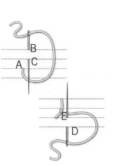

Bring the needle up at A, down at B, and up again at C, with the thread under the needle tip.

Take the needle down at D and up at E, again with the thread under the needle tip. Continue making stitches alternately up and down.

FEATHER STITCH

Another favorite of mine, this is a versatile stitch for adding detail.

Bring the needle up at A, down and B, and up at C, looping the thread under the needle tip. (The distances between A and B and B and C should be the same.)

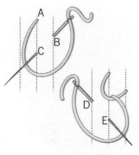

Take the needle down at D and up at E, again looping the thread under the needle tip. Continue working stitches alternately left and right.

CHEVRON STITCH

A traditional stitch that always looks great.

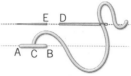

Bring the needle up at A and down at B to form a horizontal stitch. Bring the needle up at C, centered on A–B. Take the needle up to the right, insert it at D, then out at E.

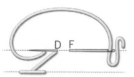

Take the needle to the right, insert it at F, then bring it out at D.

Take the needle down and insert it at G, bring it out at H, then insert it to the right, at I. Continue in the same way.

FRENCH KNOT

To get the tension right, practice these on a left-over piece of the fabric you are using for your project.

Bring the needle up at A, wrap the thread tightly around it twice, then insert the needle at A again. (You may find it easiest to hold the wraps down with the thumbnail of your non-sewing hand.) Pull the needle and the working thread slowly and carefully through the wraps to form a small knot.

FLY STITCH

These sweet little stitches can be worked singly or in groups.

Bring the needle up at A and down at B, leaving a loop of thread. Bring the needle up inside the loop at C (centred on and below A–B), and down at D, outside the loop.

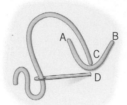

SATIN STITCH

Another classic embroidery stitch that is ever useful.

Bring the needle up at A, down at B, up at C, down at D, and so on, working the stitches close together so that no fabric shows in between them.

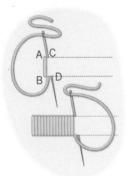

TENT STITCH

The traditional stitch for working needlepoint canvas work.

Start at the top right. Bring the needle up at A and down at B to form an upward-slanting diagonal stitch that crosses one thread intersection on the canvas, then bring the needle up at C, two vertical threads to the left and one horizontal thread down, ready to form the next stitch. Work the next row from left to right, bringing the needle up into the holes occupied by the stitches of the first row.

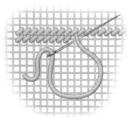

PARISIAN STITCH

This canvas stitch works up quickly and complements bargello stitch perfectly.

Begin at the top right of your work, working from right to left. Bring the needle up at A, down at B, up at C, and down at D, working alternate long and short stitches.

Work the next row from left to right, working short stitches below the long stitches of the first row and vice versa.

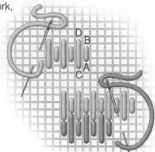

STEM STITCH

My favorite outlining stitch, this is a quick and easy stitch to work.

Bring the needle up at A, down at B, and, with the thread to the right, back up again at C, halfway between A and B. Take the needle down at D and bring it out at B, at the end of the last stitch.

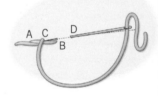

WHIPPED WHEEL

These ribbed wheels are easy to work and make for wonderful whirling eyes.

Use a fading fabric marker to draw a circle the required size and mark the center. Make six straight stitches from the edge of the circle to the middle to form a star. Bring the needle to the front just to the left of one stitch, as close as possible to the middle. Take the needle under the stitch it is closest to, then around and under that stitch again, and under the next one along in the star.

Continue around the star, taking the needle over the last stitch it came under, then back under both that stitch and the next one along. Continue around and around in this way until the spokes are completely filled in.

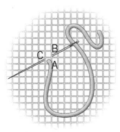

stuffing the pincushions

To make your pincushion as practical as possible, do consider what you're going to stuff it with. I recommend five different types of filling—polyester fiber, kapok, wool roving, fine sand, and carborundum grit. Each has different attributes and will suit some of the pincushions more than others. You'll find a tip box with each project telling you what I filled it with and suggesting alternative fillings if appropriate.

The best tool for stuffing corners and small shapes is a blunt-pointed knitting needle; I use an old Bakelite one. Don't use a metal or bamboo needle as they tend to be sharp-pointed and it's easy to push the needle right through the fabric of the pincushion and so ruin it. A thin chopstick makes quite a good alternative to a knitting needle.

POLYESTER FIBER STUFFING

This is widely available in craft stores and online. Buy a small bag—a little goes a long way.

This stuffing does tend to become lumpy, so pull off small pieces and fluff them up with your fingers before pushing them into the pincushion to try and make the stuffing as even and lump-free as possible. You can compress the stuffing quite a lot so the pincushion can be fairly firm, or leave it looser and spongier for a very lightweight filling.

KAPOK

As with polyester fiber, you don't need much of this to fill a pincushion.

This is a natural stuffing, the product of the seed pods of the *Ceiba pentandra* tree. It compresses beautifully, giving a firm, even filling. However, it can be a bit unruly as the very lightweight fibers float around and cling to fabrics. Despite this, I prefer it to synthetic polyester fiber.

WOOL ROVING

This is a more expensive way to fill your pincushions, but it is widely available in small amounts.

Roving is natural wool fleece and can be used in a similar way to polyester fiber; pull off and fluff up small pieces to avoid lumps. It compresses well for a firm filling and is a bit heavier than polyester fiber or kapok. This is also the material used for making felt balls in a couple of projects.

CARBORUNDUM GRIT

Also known as silicon carbide, this is an abrasive powder that will clean and sharpen your pins as you push them into to the pincushion.

You can buy this powder online, but usually only in quite large quantities. It comes in different grades and I use a 60–80 grade. It does get everywhere, so work over a sheet of newspaper. I find the best filling tool is a small, slim spoon. It makes for a very heavy, firm filling, though as it can be a bit tricky to fill the pincushion up to the very brim, I usually fill it as much as possible, then push in a little kapok (or polyester fiber or roving) to fill out the last bit of the shape.

FINE SAND

This is a more easily available alternative to carborundum grit. It will help clean and sharpen pins, but not as well as the more specialist material.

You need a fine-grain sand such as silver sand, not the type used for making cement; try aquarium suppliers as well as home improvement stores. Like carborundum, it gets everywhere and I find a spoon to be the best filling tool. Again, I find it easiest to fill out the last bit of a sand-filled pincushion with kapok.

clipping a curved seam allowance

This technique takes just a couple of minutes to do and makes a real difference to the look of your sewing as it helps curved seams lie flat.

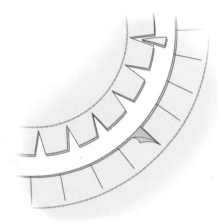

On curved seams, simply clip into the seam allowance after stitching, taking care not to cut through any of the stitches. For seams that will curve outward when turned right side out (above left), cut wedge-shaped notches; for seams that will curve inward when right side out (above right), little slits will suffice.

rouleau tube

These are easiest to make if you have a special rouleau tube turner, but you can make them using strong thread instead.

1 Cut a strip of fabric the required size. Fold it in half along its length, right sides together, and pin. Set the sewing machine to a small straight stitch. Taking a seam allowance that is about one third of the total folded width of the strip, sew along the open edge. Press the strip flat.

2 If you have a loop turner, slide it into the tube until the top emerges at the other end. Hook the latch of the turner over the end of the fabric and slowly pull it right side out. It can be tricky to get it to start turning and you may need to encourage it with your fingers.

3 If you do not have a loop turner, then cut a length of strong thread 4 in. (10 cm) longer than the strip of fabric. Fold the strip as in Step 1 and press the fold. Using a needle, secure the thread firmly to one end of the fold. Lay the rest of the thread along the fold inside the fabric strip, so the other end of the thread emerges at the other end of the strip. Stitch the seam as before, being very careful not to trap the thread in the stitching. Slowly and firmly pull on the thread to turn the tube right side out; it will almost certainly need some finger encouragement to start turning.

4 Once it is right side out, manipulate it with your fingers so that the seam runs along one edge, then press the finished tube flat.

templates

Templates are all shown at 100% and so do not have to be enlarged.

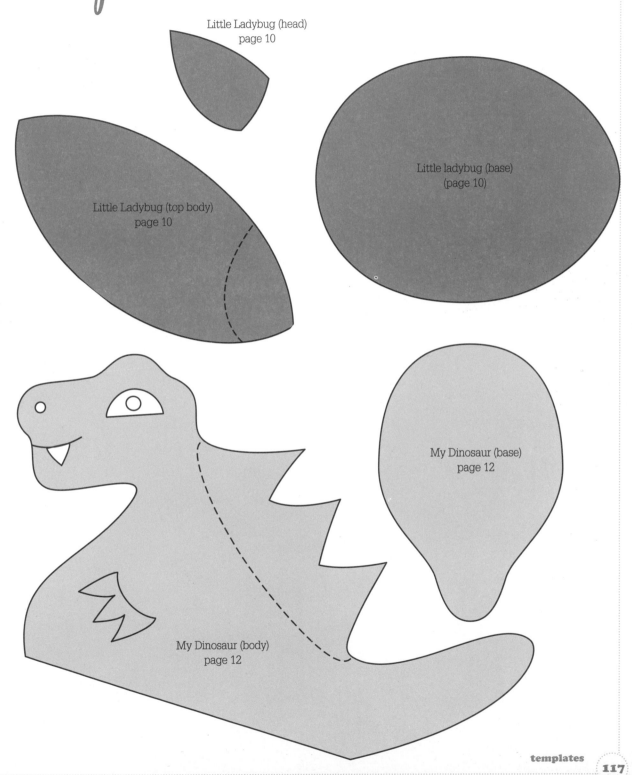

Little Ladybug (head)
page 10

Little ladybug (base)
(page 10)

Little Ladybug (top body)
page 10

My Dinosaur (base)
page 12

My Dinosaur (body)
page 12

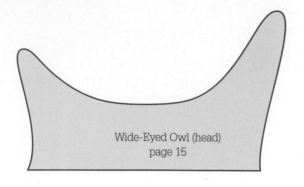

Wide-Eyed Owl (head)
page 15

Wide-Eyed Owl (beak)
page 15

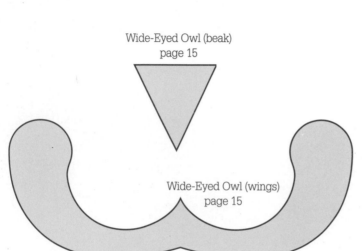

Wide-Eyed Owl (wings)
page 15

Wide-Eyed Owl (base)
page 15

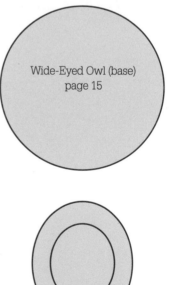

Wide-Eyed Owl (body)
page 15

Wide-Eyed Owl (eye)
page 15

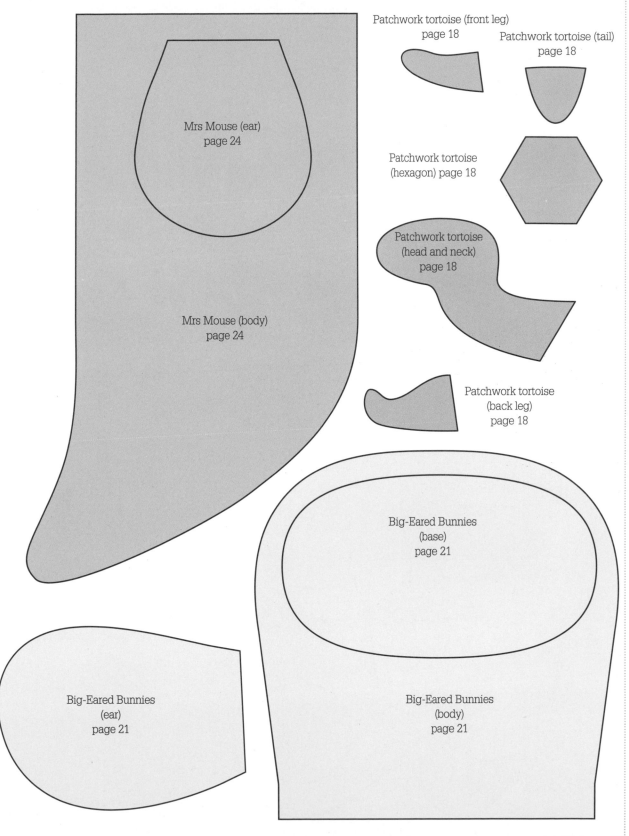

Patchwork tortoise (front leg)
page 18

Patchwork tortoise (tail)
page 18

Mrs Mouse (ear)
page 24

Patchwork tortoise
(hexagon) page 18

Patchwork tortoise
(head and neck)
page 18

Mrs Mouse (body)
page 24

Patchwork tortoise
(back leg)
page 18

Big-Eared Bunnies
(base)
page 21

Big-Eared Bunnies
(ear)
page 21

Big-Eared Bunnies
(body)
page 21

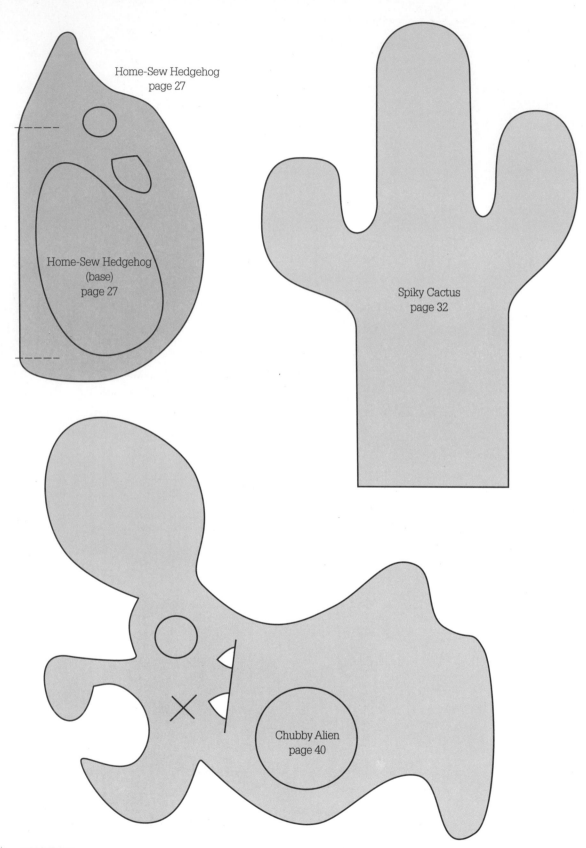

Home-Sew Hedgehog
page 27

Home-Sew Hedgehog
(base)
page 27

Spiky Cactus
page 32

Chubby Alien
page 40

Matryoshka Doll Small
page 34

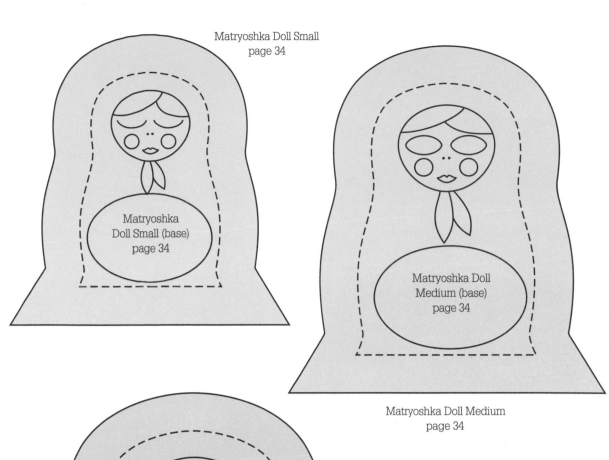

Matryoshka
Doll Small (base)
page 34

Matryoshka Doll
Medium (base)
page 34

Matryoshka Doll Medium
page 34

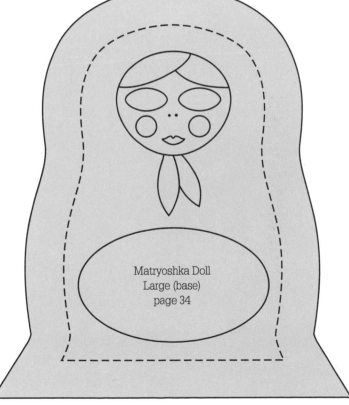

Matryoshka Doll
Large (base)
page 34

Matryoshka Doll Large
page 34

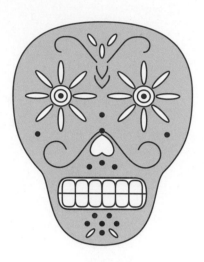

Day of the Dead
page 42

I Love Sewing
page 48

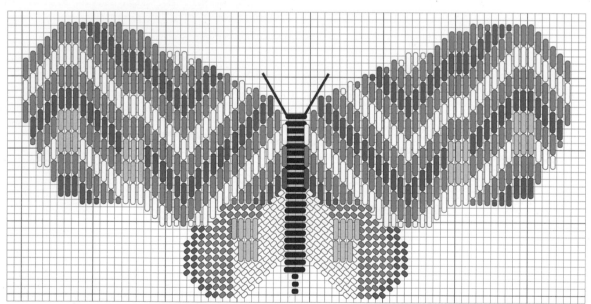

Color reference numbers for
Appleton's Crewel Wool

241   723   841

932   155   934

Bargello Butterfly
embroidery chart
page 59

Christmas Tree (heart)
page 54

Dressmaker's Watch
page 72

Pumpkin Patch (leaf)
page 92

Doughnut Pincushion
(frosting)
page 90

Toadstool (top cap)
page 95

Toadstool (bottom cap)
page 95

Toadstool (stalk)
page 95

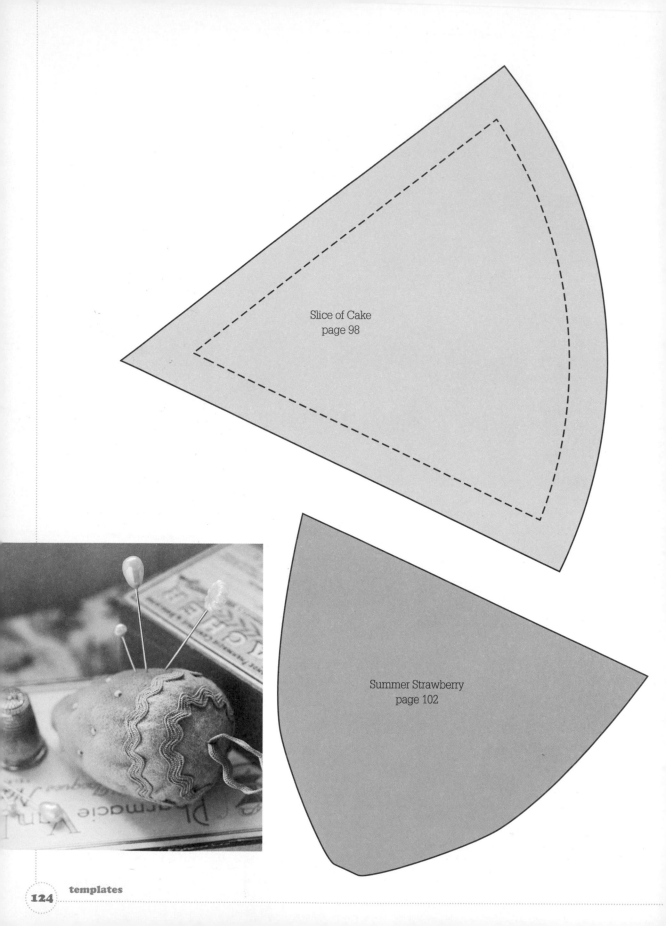

Slice of Cake
page 98

Summer Strawberry
page 102

Perfect Pear
page 105

Perfect Pear (leaf)
page 105

Peas in a
Pod (base)
page 108

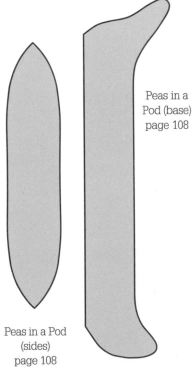

Peas in a Pod
(sides)
page 108

suppliers

US

moltingyeti on Etsy
www.etsy.com

Kapok stuffing sold by the half-pound.

Hobby Lobby
www.hobbylobby.com

Polyester fiber stuffing, plus sewing equipment, embroidery flosses (threads), and some fabrics and felts.

Joann
www.joann.com

Polyester fiber stuffing, plus sewing equipment, embroidery flosses (threads), and some fabrics and felts.

ReproductionFabrics.com
www.reproductionfabrics.com

Great range of interesting quilting fabrics.

Wool Felt Central
www.prairiepointjunction.com

Lots of colors of good-quality wool felt.

UK

Heartwood Kapok Supplies
www.heartwood2000.com

Kapok stuffing.

John Lewis
www.johnlewis.com

Polyester fiber stuffing, plus great sewing equipment and some fabrics

Liberty
www.liberty.com

Good sewing equipment and fabrics.

Creative Quilting
www.creativequilting.co.uk

Good range of fabrics and very helpful staff. Also sell some embroidery flosses (threads), wool felts, and general sewing equipment.

The Cloth House
www.clothhouse.com

My favorite fabric shop, with a range of acrylic/wool mix felts.

index

acknowledgments

At CICO, my thanks to Cindy for responding with enthusiasm to my idea for this book, to Pete for his patience and good humor in the face of all that goes wrong, and to Sally for her creative eye.

Thanks to Sarah for all her work at the editorial coalface, I do appreciate it. Thanks to Steve for illustrations that make sense AND look good, and to Mark for the excellent book design. Thanks to Sophie for the lovely styling and to Geoff, Claire, and Emma for taking equally lovely photographs.

As always, thanks to Philip for the food.